Sgt. Thomas V

C000129655

Sgt. Thomas William Chisholm
Northumberland Fusiliers
A POW Diary May 1918 – 2nd January 1919
Giessen, Darmstadt, & Lamsdorf POW Camps

Transcribed from the Sergeants diary, and compiled
with additions by his Grandson

Mike Orchard

Sgt. Thomas William Chisholm

First published in 2018 by Broomfield Publications

A catalogue record for this book is available from the British Library

ISBN 978-1-9160063-3-1

Sgt. Thomas William Chisholm

Dedication

To my Grandfather

Sgt. Thomas William Chisholm
Northumberland Fusiliers
5th Battalion
Company B
1914 -1920
Ypres
Passchendaele
The Somme
Aisne
Giessen POW Camp
Darmstadt POW Camp
Lager 3A, Barrack 126,
Lager 5
Lamsdorf O/Sch., Germany.

6th Battalion
1920 -1935

Royal Air Force
1939 – 1945

Sgt. Thomas William Chisholm

Table of Contents.

Sgt. Thomas William Chisholm

Preface

This book is the transcribed diary from WW1 as written by my grandfather Sergeant Thomas William Chisholm 1896 – 1979. Sergeant Chisholm (Bill or Will) joined the Northumberland Fusiliers in 1914, and fought at amongst others Ypres, the Somme, Paschendaele, and at the Battle of Aisne until his capture 27th May 1918. The Sergeant was then marched and railroaded in cattle trucks to many prisoner of war camps, including Giessen, Darmstadt and ultimately Lamsdorf O/Sch. where he remained until his release 1st January 1919.

My grandfather was wounded twice during his time at war, the first recorded being 25th August 1917, the second recorded as 29th November 1917. He recalls in his Diary that second wounding took place at the battle of Houlust Forest, he describes this as "a slight wound to the right knee and upper lip", which may account for him always having a moustache.

He was not demobbed from the 5th Battalion N/land Fusiliers until April 1920, when he immediately rejoined the 6th Battalion Northumberland Fusiliers and rose to Company Sergeant Major, He retired from them in 1935 when he was presented with an engraved mantle clock, which continues to be used by his family to this day.

Sgt. Thomas William Chisholm

His great grandson (whom he did get to meet before he passed away in 1979) also joined the Fusiliers many years after his passing.

Four years after his retirement my Grandfather tried to join the N/land Fusiliers again, when his old foe who was also involved in the 3rd battle of Aisne (a certain Adolf Hitler) decided to have another go at him. This time the Fusiliers decided he was too old for action, so he joined the RAF as a Flight Sergeant. As far as I know he served with the RAF locally during the war, by way of his involvement at home in Newcastle with the placement of the local barrage balloons.

At the end of WW2, he went back to the N/land Fusiliers and I can remember him as being generally known to be either in his garden which he loved or "at the drill hall" right up to through the, fifties and early sixties.

My grandfather was a highly respected man by all who knew and met him, he married shortly after WW1 and had two daughters, three grandchildren and eight great grandchildren My grandmother passed away a few years before him, in January 1973 and he passed away in the Freeman Hospital in April

1979, but remained very much a Company Sergeant Major to that day.

Sgt. Thomas William Chisholm

My grandfathers Diary has been transcribed from his original writing, and is presented therefore as he wrote it.

The first section of the diary gives the reader information about his arrival in and around the area which the battle of Aisne took place. The lead up to, and including the battle, his capture, and his onward journey and subsequent life as a prisoner of war, until his eventual release in January 1919

Sgt. Thomas William Chisholm

Acknowledgements:

The postcards included on the front and rear covers, as well as in the body of the book, were donated by my mother, many years ago along with a typed version of the diary to The Fusilier Museum of Northumberland at Alnwick Castle. They appear here with the kind permission of the Fusilier Museum of Northumberland.

The Front and Rear cover pages were designed and produced by my very good friend Brian (Jack) B. Burness at Flying Colours Print Room. Thanks Jack.

Sgt. Thomas William Chisholm

Chapter 1

The Advanced Party.

Somewhere in the vicinity of the 5th May 1918, I with many others was chosen to go in advance as assistants to our G.Q.M.S. (Company Quarter Master Sergeant). We were supplied with service bicycles, which are the most unwieldy article in the service, together with F.M.O and rifles, and extra rations to last us about two days, with orders to meet and entrain at a certain point namely Aire.

We completed this movement under great difficulty, owing to being hampered with so much kit, but the formidable Northumbrian spirit kept us on the alert for what was going to happen next.

When we did meet up with the train we discovered that there was no carriages to travel in, so we just had to make the best of it on the open trucks, underneath our own transport wagon which had been put aboard at Whitby camp prior to our leaving.

We scrambled aboard, about eight men to a truck and eventually rumbled away to god knows where. We travelled for about two days and nights in this fashion, our food consisted of cold pork and beans, bread, bully beef, and whenever the train happened to come to a standstill, we all made a wild dash for the engine for a supply of hot water with which to make some tea, but having used our supply on the second day we broke into the iron rations, which eventually caused some trouble when our destination was reached.

Towards the evening of the second day we came to a standstill just outside Paris, but had to be content with a view of the railway sidings and the suburbs of the city, because we were never sure when this old train with square wheels would start again. We rode throughout the night with the bitterly cold winds blowing between the spokes of the wheels of the wagons, huddled together with great coats and ground sheets wrapped round to try and keep as much warmth as possible, but it was no good we shivered like aspen leaves.

Arriving at our destination Fere-en-Tardenois we heaved a sigh of relief and commenced the tramp to take over the part of the line we were to occupy from the French troops. Arriving at the village of Pontavert during the heat of the day, we handed in our bicycles and formally took over a series of hutments, and occupied the same until the next morning (approx 9th May), when we were early astir and having partaken of a good breakfast, moved off towards the general reserve line situated in the village of Concevreux. We did not linger very long here as it was only necessary to have the various billets pointed out, so moving further afield we came to more or less rather open country. Being the height of summer everything seemed to be at its very best. The trees were beautiful and fresh with their coats of green and the grass reminded one of the beautiful downs in the south of England.

This road appeared to be the main artery between Fismes and Reims, running parallel with the River Aisne for a considerable distance, but between Concevreux and what was to be our next camp as it was called, was a beaten track across country between the river and the main road. Whilst crossing this track we could see good distance to the right towards the line. About two hundred yards in front, was low lying ground (untouched by the ravaging gunfire and smothered with green grass and poppies) also forming a natural basin, where in wet weather must by appearances, be subject to flooding. A trestle bridge ran from river to road, which in such weather would enable anyone to move across country by a very short route. Looking further ahead we could see a wrecked village just beyond a small wood, behind this wood was a small cemetery containing something like three hundred graves. At the entrance of this was a large crucifix which was discernible from practically any point within a three mile radius.

Continuing along the main road towards the Bois de Butte, which turned out to be a real nest of French 75's, and anti tank guns, on our extreme left was the California Plateau towering high above everything with its flat top. However we were not destined to touch that piece of land until a later date, so we continued towards the Bois de Butte. Upon our arrival we were received by two very smart French Officers, who looked as if they had just stepped out of a band box, they were so very clean and spruce. Not being able to speak or understand any of their language I had to be content with just following them around this natural fort, glancing occasionally at the map in the officer's possession and picking out the lay of the land that lay in front.

All in all I think there were about eighteen to twenty 75lb guns on and around this small hill with its innocent wooded slopes, the guns being cleverly camouflaged and the living quarters for the men were the essence of comfort. Having duly looked over this piece of ground we looked to our front and support lines. This part of the country being of a chalky nature the trenches were easily picked out. Straight in front was a village very much knocked about, but one could see working parties moving in and out amongst its ruins in daylight which very much amused our party, because on any other part of the front one dared not show so much as a finger.

Of course the more we were seeing of this the more we were liking it, as it looked what it was meant to be for us, a proper rest camp, but little did we know our pleasure was to be so short lived..

After reviewing all of this and taking in all the main landmarks, including two wrecked French tanks half left of this position, it was time to get back to our billets for the night, because we had about six miles to go back to them. It was beginning to get dark and through all this time we had not heard a shot fired, so with pleasant thought of a good supper and a bottle of good champagne (at two francs a bottle by the way) we turned in for the night in readiness for next morning, when our last day of the advanced party would end and the Battalion would arrive.

Reveille was at five am next morning, so we hurriedly dressed, breakfasted and putting on just a bandolier containing fifty rounds of ammunition, rifle, steel helmet and box respirator, marched off about 06:45 for the support and front lines. We traversed the same ground as the previous day, but continued on past the Bois de Butte and on into the village, then branched off to the left and entered a communications trench dug out of chalk.

Continuing through this veritable maze we eventually arrived at a small wood in a hollow, splendid to gaze upon. There were various sandbag erections with elephant iron roofs very carefully camouflaged (just outside of these were roughly made tables and forms made from branches of trees and all of this nicely placed so as to be away from aircraft observations) under the welcome shade of overhanging branches of huge trees which sheltered the tables from the glare of the hot sun.

Then commenced the proper job of taking over, whilst the officers commanding the British went about with the French men, we juniors, with the company of the French sergeants dived down into the funk holes, or deep dugouts. About thirty feet down earthen stairs, well built up at the sides to stop the earth from falling in, we arrived at the bottom, to come into the dugout proper, with its long passage and cubby holes running into the sides, containing properly made wooden bunks lit by electric light. When this failed the French had not been idle, as hanging from the sides of their bunks were small lamps made from their own egg bombs resting in wire sockets. There was also a good supply of rubber boots to be used in wet weather. Altogether things seemed to look very bright for us in the future.

On coming to ground level again by our officer, and he pointed out just where the dynamo house and Company Head Quarters were. That completed, we were preparing to go back again, when a sergeant of the French troops who could speak fairly good English, asked if we would care to stay for dinner. Naturally it was accepted on the spot, so we wiled away the time looking over the ground in the vicinity.

On getting away from the huts into the wood we found lilies of the valley growing in great numbers and the scent was just splendid, however, in the distance we heard a call and returned to find dinner richly spread on the tables already mentioned under the trees. We started off with soup, then, fish caught in the river, followed by very small potatoes boiled nicely in fat, cabbage, and a dish containing what looked like shrimps beautifully cooked and brown, to which we took a liberal helping and thoroughly enjoyed the same.

Nothing was said until it was all over. We were partaking of wine and champagne, when our host turned to us with a broad grin on his face, and asked us if we had realized what we had just eaten. "Of course" I said "shrimps", our C.Q.M.S said winkles, and that made them all laugh out loud. "No" he said "you have just eaten a plate of snails." Well to say the least we were all petrified, however we were obliged to admit that it was one of the most palatable dishes we had had for some time, so we sat talking and drinking until the sun began to cool, then we decided it was time to get back to our billets in Concevreux. That however that was easier said than done, for it was quite evident that we had dined too well. I will not describe the journey

16

back as it can better be imagined. Let it suffice to say that I and my pal Fred, arrived very tired and foot sore somewhere about 6am, and all being quiet we sneaked into bed so no one was any the wiser as to what time we got in.

Chapter 2

The Battalion, Battle, & Captivity

The Battalion duly arrived, and there were greetings of 'What's it like here? Is the line very far? Does he shell very much?' and when everything had been fully explained, the boys were more or less contented. Then started the work of issuing blankets etc, and the hundred and one things that are required, one of the chief things being a supply of ammunition, because there was hardly any in this district excepting French stuff and that was no good to use in our rifles.

With everything done, guards posted, pickets detailed, alarm post chosen, the boys as usual went out on the scrounge for foods such as egg and chips, steak and chips and the usual beer shops. I'm afraid the beer shops did very little trade when it was discovered that champagne could be bought for two francs a bottle. However there was so much consumed that the locals soon jumped the price and within a few days it was fifteen francs a bottle.

The boys still thought it was home from home, and all went pretty well during our tour in the support and front lines until we were relieved by the 6th Battalion on or about the 18th May 1018. We took our four days rest back in Concevreux, but on the afternoon of the Sunday 26th an all present parade was called. Extra ammunition supplies were issued and we were told that an attack was expected to take place at 1am Monday 27th. We were told where the alarm post was to be and that no one was allowed out of the billets. This done the company was dismissed and we settled down to talk of what and how it was going to happen.

Things were exceedingly quiet, like the lull before the storm, until somewhere about 09:00 – 09:30pm our batteries opened fire on their points of concentration and approaches, but no one replied to this fire. Our guns kept up the harassing fire until midnight when they quietened down a little bit. By this time the whole Battalion were on alarm waiting for what was going to happen next. Officers rushed about giving final instructions to senior N.C.O's as to what formation to adopt and the route to be taken, and positions to be taken up. Transport wagons had taken some of the surplus equipment away, but a good deal was still left behind including my chest, containing about four pairs of good homemade socks, towel, great coat and some rather valuable papers which I used on a course of instruction at the 8th Corps. School. Well we were all stood changing from one foot to the other and talking with hushed voices and waiting patiently for the next move, and it came suddenly, for almost dead on the

19

minute we heard the whiz and plop of two gas shells just in front of the form we had vacated, and almost immediately it seemed that the whole German artillery opened fire. The air was filled with shrieking, and groaning, shells and the crash and crump of the explosions were terrifying. However we stood our ground awaiting orders, which eventually came and it was to don gas masks, and move into the open, as the main street in any village was always a mark for a gunner. This bombardment went on all night as we waited for further orders.

Sgt. Thomas William Chisholm

Monday 27th May 1918

There were very few casualties considering the shell fire, but the main part had been dumped on the front and support lines. The wind blowing gently from the direction of the enemy lines reeked of powder and the sickly tang of gas.

By this time about 3am our gas masks were in a bad state, the glasses were dimmed with perspiration and the waterproof bag covering was sticking to our faces and very wet, but we dare not move them owing to the risk of getting a dose of the poison. This confinement was the worst part of it because anyone who has had to wear one will know how difficult it is to breath.

Somewhere near 8am our Company Commander decided to move forward, so we headed for the cross country track so well known to us, towards the road. But this was out of the question, because it was absolutely being plastered with all sorts of iron work, and a fly could not live on it, so we were content with moving across the piece of dead ground between Concevreux and the French cemetery, it being fairly well left alone. We succeeded in reaching the rear side of the cemetery and skirted round the left side nearest the road, when suddenly the enemy barrage lifted, and seemed to drop right amongst us. Then it was for who could get forward the quickest. Earth, smoke, and the moans and yells all mingled with the deepening crashes of bursting shells tended to make everyone get behind even a blade of grass.

Finally we scrambled through the cemetery and moved about thirty to forty yards in front and proceeded to dig in with as much speed as we could, because by this time we were under distant machine gun fire as well. Things were getting rather warm and unpleasant, and owing to the smoke and the morning haze visibility was very bad, and gas masks made it much worse. Being a platoon commander I tried to marshal my men into some kind of formation, and issued instructions with regard to entrenchments and they worked like Trojans

Inside half an hour they were fairly well off under the circumstances, in regard to cover, my orderly stuck to me very well and was remarkably cool, owing to the fact that this was the first big fight he had taken part in. He had just been transferred from R.F.C and was really too young to be where he was, so I decided to take him under my wing to save him more or less from the arduous duties of the trench.

By this time the sun was fairly well up and the heat was beginning to make itself felt. The time being somewhere about 9am we were just feeling a little bit hungry, and the men were asking when it would be possible to get something to eat, when suddenly to my surprise we were hailed from the road which lay on our left and lo and behold there were the cooks with their field kitchen with smoke pouring out of the chimneys. To say the least it was a shock to see them, as it seemed an almost impossible thing for anything to move up that road. Never the less they were there and the greeting they gave us was "Howay get all this stuff off. Do ye want us to all get blown to hell standin' here all day?" So I called for volunteers which soon came in the form of eight men and with a mad rush we snatched up all the dishes and made back for the trenches. I managed to get hold of the bacon and forthwith proceeded to dish it out with my hand. The grease had become cold, and it was almost hard, but we could pick out the bacon from the fat. I offered some to the O.C Coy but the sight of the cold fat turned him against it. I think he decided that a little libation from his flask would be more beneficial.

At this point in the distance, suddenly we observed two dispatch riders on motorcycles literally tearing up the road towards the front line, (which had already been pierced) and were in grave danger of running into the enemy line, so we hailed them to stop, and when told of the position, they soon turned about and made back towards Head Quarters. They only got about quarter of a mile back when their machines were blown from under them and they were killed.

We got something to fire at, but after killing one or two, owing to the haze it was discovered that they were French troops.

A CSM of the Durham dashed over and reported that the Germans were getting round the wood on our left but the OC Coy denied this and told him to go to hell (personally I thought we were there already).

By 9:45am they were well advanced, and on looking behind through the information of my pal Fred, it was to see two scouts come out from behind the wood, followed by his machine gun teams, then there was a scramble to get back, but it was pretty hopeless from the first. I called my platoon to follow me, as there was still a chance to get clear, so taking a course straight through the cemetery directly behind, we dodged amongst the graves and head stones as quickly as it was possible, because the bullets from both rifles and machine guns were coming like hail amongst us, but we were rather lucky with regard to casualties as there were very few hit, but some had been killed outright, and so far as I could gather about three of the boys wounded, including my batman and runner through the left shoulder. On reaching lower ground these were dressed and we made straight for the River Vesle, where there were bridges at intervals. We scurried forward, but when we were about a hundred yards from the first bridge, a deafening report rent the air and our hopes were dashed as the bridge went skywards in a million pieces. Not daunted we made along the river bank towards the next one but our Royal Engineers were doing their work thoroughly and up went another three. There was nothing left to do but stand fast and await events.

The heat was almost overpowering, when an officer, one of the platoon commanders came forward to me to enquire as to what I thought we had better do next. On going through the trees which lined the river bank, we saw a rare sight and soon drew back under cover again to hold a short consultation. In the end he wanted to reorganize and make a bayonet charge, but that solution was out of the question, owing to the fact that on the other side of the trees were something like three hundred disarmed British troops being covered with three machine guns and three flame throwers or liquid fire machines, so any attempt at attack would have meant wholesale slaughter of all those men. I gave him my opinion, and acted upon it without his permission. In fact I ordered him to dump his revolver and equipment in the River Vesle and keep only what was required for personal use. The Lewis guns I had brought forward and placed on the ground, put a couple of rounds through the machine and pitched into the air. This part of the program completed, we rather gingerly moved once more through the trees into the open, where all the captives we being horded together like a lot of terrified sheep, not knowing what was going to happen next. Also the very piece of ground I have already mentioned as the natural basin, but the position of the troops being reversed, the enemy having a strong advantage over us, by having his formidable weapons mounted on the long wood trestle bridge, which being at a height just suitable for a massacre should his gunners and fire operators desire, which I may say, was expected any second. Owing to our numbers, it was thought that they would not trouble to take us prisoners.

Meanwhile his troops were trying to get something like five to six hundred British on to the bridge, and when it began to creak and crack, there was a panic so he decided it would be better to form up on terra firma and march us onto the main road.

Chapter 3

Captivity and a Forced March.

The time being about noon judging by the position of the sun, we were unceremoniously formed into fours on the main road and moving in the direction of Guignicourt.

We had proceeded for about quarter of a mile, passing through the enemy lines of advancing troops. First came his infantry, followed by light mortars, heavy mortars, machine guns, pioneers filling up all shell holes as they came forward to enable the transport to come in comfort along the roads. Next came medical services, followed by fairly solid lines of artillery in order of merit, light field guns, howitzers, then all his heavy guns, and coming pretty close again were the observation sections mounted on motor lorries. The wheels of these lorries were not tyred in the usual way with rubber, but round the rim was a series of coil springs kept in place by an outer tyre of flat steel band, thus when moving over rough surfaces these springs could take the shock and jolt similar but not so good as the rubber tyre. Above us were the huge sausage shaped balloons hundreds of feet in the air watching with all eyes, the advance in the forward areas.

One incident which happened goes to prove some of the almost unbelievable atrocities which the enemy committed during the war and a few of our boys being almost in the rear of the column witnessed it without being able to give a helping hand so just had to bear it and keep moving.

It was when their Red Cross men were coming over the ground passing our killed and wounded and not offering to give a hand to relieve their sufferings in the least. (I might mention before going any further that these supposed Red Cross people who unlike our R.Q.M.C., were armed with an automatic revolver, cartridge pouch and bayonet.) This particular German walked over to a man lying with his guts hanging out having been hit with a piece of flying shell, the man was doomed in the first place as it was really no good trying to patch him up, but the German walked up to him, and trying to raise himself on one arm asked for water. The swine just shook his head saying 'Nein, nein, nein nix wasser.'. The tommy, who was a Durham man opened his breast pocket, took out his wallet and offered him a fifty franc note, again gasping out 'Water, water.'. At this the Gerry took everything from him and drawing his bayonet, slashed him across the mouth. The man then lost consciousness and with a howl, we started forward to attack but being without arms we could do nothing and our guards, for there were plenty of them and big ones at that, with a yell of "Rouse!" or words meaning to 'get back', we could do nothing but grit our teeth and with a few curses the German moved on his way, and we were marched in the opposite direction. We never saw our comrade no more, for he was sure to die a brutal and inhuman death.

We continued our journey along the river road and three hundred yards further on came across some of his General Staff mounted on horse-back. One gentleman in particular, having under his arm an English loaf of bread and a jar of jam. It seems hard to believe, but never the less quite true. There he sat watching prisoners move past, and he, every now and then tearing a handful of bread would dip it into the jam, and eat as if his very life depended upon it.

Another quarter of a mile or so and we were passing in the shadow of the great California Plateau, and on looking up to the top most point we could see a crowd of German officers and a few yards ahead of them there was standing a solitary man standing with his cape gently blowing in the breeze. This man proved later to be the great War Lord of Germany, the Kaiser himself watching his troops doing their work of destruction as they moved forward.

The heat of the day was at it's worst now and we were beginning to feel the effects and wondering when we were going to get a halt and something to eat because the last good meal we had was about 4:30pm on Sunday afternoon and it was now 2:30pm on Monday. We had no water either to fall back on as a reserve, having dumped all before being taken, so we just trudged along, Fred No 1 on the right, myself on the left and being supported by us was Fred No 2 my batman, as we had to carry our own wounded, and with no idea where we were bound for, what with our sore feet, parched throats, the heat together with the groans from Fred 2 it was a very unpleasant position to be in. Fred 1 cursed the square head fluently all the way.

This continued until 6:30pm without a spell, when we arrived at a fairly large barbed wire compound and being counted when passing through the gate, all this done the gate was securely locked and surrounded by guards. On looking round there was no chance of escape.

Next we were fed our first meal in captivity, which brought it's own problem. Having no small kit what, were we going to get this meal in, and what to eat it with? Fred 1 came to the rescue. Taking off his steel helmet, he tore out the lining and low and behold there was as good a soup bowl as one could wish to have. Many followed likewise and forming up in the line, arrived at the boiler from which a German with a litre measure dished out a white liquid, which turned out to be nothing else but flour and water boiled, so putting our helmets to our lips we drank deeply. Hardly had this been done when we were moved into a more remote corner of the compound for the night, and it was a cold one.

Everyone huddled together in the open, without any sort of covering, in an endeavour to keep warm. The outside men, one of them being me, had to keep turning over from back to front as required.

So ended the 27th May as my first day as a prisoner of war.

Sgt. Thomas William Chisholm

Wednesday 28th May 1918

At 5:30am the rouse came again, and with another drink of flour and water we were turned into a large field just over the other side of the hill. When this was done Fred 1 said 'I wonder what they are going to do now Bill.' 'God knows, and he won't split.' said I.

Sitting for a short while we watched Jerry's movements, until Fred 1 said 'Billy if you want to keep anything you value get it smuggled quick because they are searching every man.' It had to be done under cover because Jerry was watching with an eagle eye, so covering each others movements, we transferred each article we wished to keep, down inside our trousers, or in our boots. I happened to have in my possession four one mark notes, having taken them from a Jerry prisoner in a previous engagement, so Fred says 'For goodness sake get rid of them or when they see them your days are numbered,' so with my jackknife I dug a small hole in the ground and buried them, and with a sigh of relief joined the line to be searched.

The number to be searched being so large, it was surprising that the searching was such a short affair. When we had passed through we were minus our jackknives, and any other small articles that would be of any use to our guards. This being done we found ourselves on the road to God knows where, the order was given to march so off the column trudged, the time being about 10am.

After about four spells that day we came to a place called Lislet. It boasted a proper prison camp, and all were put into huts no matter what rank they held. By the time this was done it was 10:30pm and this practically ended our second day as prisoners. The huts were fairly large and roomy, but they were packed to suffocation, however it was much better than being out in the open. The camp being a big one was built in the form of a hollow square and surrounded by a double wall of barbed wire twelve feet high. Outside this was a small embankment four feet above ground level which was used by our guards as their beat and they had to walk up and down towards each other.

By 12pm all was quiet, as we were dead tired and needed as much sleep as possible, owing to the fact that we did not know what the morrow would bring. About 2am we were awakened by a loud whirring sound, so going outside to investigate, I found out that our aircraft were on the way and it proved quite true because when they came overhead and dropped their first bomb Jerry disappeared with a squeal and we saw no more of them until the raid was over. That caused us to get a good strapping from Jerry next day.

We rested two days in the camp. All there was to do was just walk round and get in touch with a few of the boys we had not seen since our capture, and feed upon the soup very kindly given to us by Jerry with the intention of keeping us alive, but it was really just a long drink. We were also given a small piece of black bread. We looked at each other before starting to eat, Fred and I thought we would sample ours but owing to its bitterness we could not finish it, but some of the less particular of the boys made short work of it..

By this time my wounded batman Fred 2 had been taken away from the party and put in a hospital somewhere. Whatever happened to him I never knew for he was never seen again

This camp and the rest seemed to do us a good deal of good, but being unable to either wash or shave, we did look a grubby crowd. On the second day I happened to meet my old Company Commander who seemed in a very cheerful mood. We had a good chat over past events and parted, to see no more of each other until about twelve months after I returned to England.

That brought the day to the 31st May 1918, a Friday, and rumours that night, that we were to move again on the morrow.

Chapter 4

Onward to Giessen via Fort de Hirson.

Saturday 1st June 1918

Up at 4am and after partaking of coffee and black bread we marched off again, this time under the charge of a guard of stalwart but rather old Prussian Guards mounted on very pristine horses who continued to trot backwards and forwards along the column keeping a very sharp eye on all that happened.

Getting on for about noon this day, the column were passing through a series of small villages, and by this time, we were again in no fit state to march so far without a break, but our guards kept us on the move all the time. Owing to the bad state of the roads and intense heat, we were all covered with a good coating of white dust, with streaks down our faces where the perspiration had been running down. Our mouths parched with thirst, sore feet, stiff limbs and sick of heart through this heartless treatment, we were passing through the village of Liart. The peasants noticed our plight and seemed to take pity on us, as they put outside the houses, small wooden tubs of clean fresh water for drinking. Without attempting at any halt to enable us to refresh ourselves, our guards rode forward and willfully turned over the tubs and forced us back into the ranks again. We just trudged forward very little being said, owing I think, to the fact that we wanted to save our breath as much as possible for our exertions.

We continued moving past fields looking more cultivated than the ones we had left behind, and great woods of giant fir trees. The time was somewhere about 6:30 or 7pm, when we suddenly left the road and entered one of these dense woods. Moving across a beaten track, we continued for something like half an hour before coming into the open again. Then across country for about half a mile and then came to a halt.

We had arrived at Hirson, a fairly large French town dominated by a fortress on the Borden. It was into this, that we were to rest for the next 24 hours. The Fort de Hirson, being surrounded by walls built of huge pieces of rock, this retaining wall afforded very little chance of escape. Also last but not least a large moat about 35 to 40 feet deep and 30 feet across the top.

The time being somewhere about 7.30pm, the light had not begun to fail yet so we to set off to explore our prison, in an effort to find a decent resting place, before dark came upon us. Wherever we looked, it was all the same, great towering walls faced us, so we just had to be content with a place against the wall, wherever a space could be found. Just imagine what it would be like when something like 8 or 9 hundred people tried to line a wall and find a comfortable place to lie.

Fred and I squatted down in a place as near as possible to the entrance thinking of an early exit next morning. Hunger was growing at our stomachs as we had had nothing to eat all day and it looked as if nothing was forthcoming. Even if we could have got a smoke it would have been better than nothing, but not being in the possession of the necessary articles, we had to do without. Fred however, was not to be outdone. Having a supply of cigarette papers, as he always did make his own cigs (like all men in the service of the merchant marine) finding a large heap of the refuse in one corner of the moat, being a dump used by the Germans, for all scrap such as potato skins, tea leaves etc., Fred managed to manufacture a cigarette by using the tea leaves and powdered dry grass. As for myself I usually smoked a pipe, so I properly filled up and smoked, but the taste and smell was nothing on earth, however I stuck at it until satisfied.

All this time the people up above (French and German sight seers), who had turned out in full force to see such a large batch of British prisoners, were talking among themselves and occasionally jibing at us, intending I suppose, in making us feel our position a little more acute. So when we did understand anything that was said, it did not take long for us to give them a suitable answer, which was not always in the best of English language (some people call it "choice").

Our visitors keep tormenting our hunger, by displaying large pieces of sausage, bananas, and black bread, but by only dropping the skins into the moat, they seemed to enjoy seeing the boys make a rush for them. Personally I have never been nearer to being an animal than at this particular period. All that we wished for, was that we had been shot dead in the first place.

Eventually with the darkness, the crowd up above drifted away, and quietude rained.

Sgt. Thomas William Chisholm

Sunday 2nd June 1918

The day passed without event, and on the night all that could be seen or heard, was the sentries feet and the figures of the guards moving along the stone coping round the top of our prison, and the groups of prisoners down below, on their damp cold ground beds, talking about anything that seemed to come into their heads.

Some talked of home and what their people would have to say when they heard of their sons or fathers plight. Others grumbled at the hunger and the cold, whilst some even tried to brighten our burden by singing the war marches that we had sung during happier days.

Eventually all was silent and the more contented slept fitfully throughout the night (which now seems a nightmare after all these years, but is as fresh in my memory as if it had happened last week).

Monday 3rd June 1918

Morning came bright and fresh, but no grub. At about 7am we were all hustled out of the hell hole to a railway station and put aboard the train and rolled away again, arriving about 3.30pm at the town of Giessen.

Detraining here, we marched through the streets to the other side of the town and were put into a real and proper prison camp, which was fairly large, containing good huts.

During our march through the town, we noticed the streets were spotlessly clean, also proving as to what a state of depression and starvation the German nation had been reduced to, we noticed in a few instances confessionary shop windows with not the usual display of goods, but in their place were coffins, also in drapers, and bakers shops, the same thing meet our gaze.

We were met at the entrance to the camp by other prisoners who had been in captivity a good while, but who also looked as if it had done them good. They had a well fed appearance and were very well clothed, being dressed in the regulation uniform prescribed for British prisoners of war. It was made of the same material as our usual service dress, only it was dyed black with a brown band around the right arm and a two inch brown strip down the sides of the trousers. Not having seen this before, we decided it looked rather funny, but all the same, comfortable, seeing as by this time our own uniforms were looking and feeling the worse for wear.

These men who had been prisoners for a considerable period welcomed us with the news that there was a feed ready for us. I might say that we all seemed as though we needed one, judging by our friend's appearance, because he did look well fed.

As soon as we were put into our various barracks, the food was brought and placed between the huts, where we all formed into eager queues and a German Pastern or sentry issued out the soup with a litre ladle with a handle about four feet long. As soon as a man obtained his portion, he returned to the hut to which he belonged, to partake of the first substantial meal we had had for days, which also proved very much insufficient, for our most starved condition however, it had to do, as there was no more to get.

Following this meal we were again turned out on parade and this time an RSM who had previously belonged to the Rifle Brigade carried out a nominal roll of all men in our batch. That is the only name it is possible to find for such a mixed crowd.

Followed by the RSM, came a German officer with his followers, he spoke very good English, so before ever he got anywhere near to where Fred and I were, it was passed up the ranks that he was making enquiries with regard to what trade we worked at before the war, and also that he seemed to splitting us into distinct parties. Fred and I having being pals so long now, we did not feel inclined to part, and thinking that this officer was looking for tradesmen with a view to placing us in his factories, thus relieving more German soldiers to go to the front. Fred and I had a little talk and decided that I was to tell them that my trade was a blacksmith and also that Fred had in peace times, been my striker, although he had really never seen inside of a blacksmith's shop. Nevertheless the gag worked and we were both put into the squad containing such tradesman as engineers, both mechanical and electrical, boilermakers, blacksmiths and motor mechanics etc., so we felt fairly safe for the time being.

When all this had been done, the complete roll was called, and not being content with this, the officer and the German Sgt. Major counted us three times in succession to make sure that it corresponded with his numbers in the first place, and the roll that the British RSM had made, ensuring that no one had escaped during the journey.

Finally the dismissal came and we were told that another meal would be forthcoming somewhere about 10.00pm but it never came yet, so we laid down each beneath his one blanket and slept a good sound sleep, also the first of its kind, as up till now we had to sleep without any covering at all.

This ended June 3rd 1918.

Sgt. Thomas William Chisholm

This is the registration document eventually entered for the Sergeants arrival at Giessen POW Camp.

Chapter 5

Off Again & Onward to Darmstadt POW.

Tuesday 4th June 1918

Up and about by 5am after a meal of what was called breakfast composed of soup of a dark brown colour in which was floating a few grains of burnt barley. We didn't want much of this as it tasted so bitter and what our guards called coffee, never the less it had to go down with a portion of black bread.

After this we fell in and were counted, the roll called and finally marched off to the railway station to be crammed into 3rd class carriages and puffed out of the station, on another stage of our eventful journey.

By this time it seemed evident that we were doomed to keep moving about like this for the remainder of the war. We had a stop at Frankfurt for two hours to wait for another train to complete the journey. We were taken into a small restaurant in which were a few old Germans who we were told were being called up by their class. There did not seem to be very much food in this place, as all we could see these uniforms were being supplied with, was roast potatoes. One old man seemingly must have took pity on us seeing our ragged clothes and bare feet, smuggled a few potatoes in his pocket and when he was leaving, edged close to the table where we were seated and so as not to be seen, quietly dropped them onto my lap and walked out as if nothing had occurred. I quickly transferred them to my pocket for a foreseeable opportunity, but that did not come until we boarded our next train.

A surprise awaited us on arrival at the next stop (which proved to be for a period of a month). The place by the name of Darmstadt, seemed a town of fairly big dimensions and as in the best place very clean.

We formed up on the station platform and were once again counted, formed fours to the right and stood waiting the signal from our guard commander to move ahead.

These guards we a little different class of men than had previously been in charge of us, not the usual square headed, robust German we had been used to seeing, but a class of men who seemed only fit for home service duties and who seemed rather old to be in uniforms at all. I think I heard someone call them Landstrums, however they were remarkably kind and talkative to us which was rather notable. The previous ones were sullen and inclined to bully and beat us on the slightest provocation.

Finally the column moved off and after half an hour or so arrived at the camp gates surrounded by a high barrier of barbed wire. As we passed through the sentries and an officer counted once again. It was getting a bit of a joke now because as soon as the boys saw that the counting was about to commence someone would strike up with that well known hymn "Count Your Morning Blessings", not that we were any blessing to Gerry. Only in one way, as we were the cause of giving a good number of them nice cushy jobs. "Well, well, ye Gods and little fishes, where are we Fred? Is this going to be our permanent billet?" I think Fred was too overcome to answer me, he just stood and stared round the room we had been put into. It was a stoutly built building, similar in appearance to a large cricket pavilion, with heavy rafters across and supporting the sloping roof, fairly high, walls being made of wood, one piece overlapping the other, plenty of windows with ventilation and above all it was beautifully stained and varnished. Round the walls were bunks in tiers of three of two with room for six men to one set. About fifty were put into this hut, Fred and I claiming one of these bunks in the centre of the floor.

After ten minutes of being in here a German Sergeant Major came in and kindly asked if we were hungry and said a good meal would be forthcoming very soon. He also made enquiries as to whether we had been able to write home and tell our people where we were. On being told that had been impossible up to present, he volunteered to supply us with paper and envelopes, and promised to see that our letters were posted by the next mail (our people never got those letters).

However, in came the promised meal consisting of a good portion of bread, tinned meat of some sort, and some real good coffee. If we wanted any more we just had to ask for it. After a good tuck in we started to think then of a wash, the Sergeant Major having detailed a corporal and a sergeant to look after our most pressing needs, of course not being in possession of a razor, a shave was out of the question, so after a good bath it was then just about time to retire, which all seemed rather anxious to do. After getting snuggled down amongst our three blankets, in came some more coffee as a nightcap.

Well this all seemed to good to be true, but all the time it was true so after running about half naked in the business of getting more coffee we finally got down to it for the night and slept the sleep of the just.

Wednesday 5th June 1918

The morning came as any fine morning could be expected to do, beautifully warm and sunny and breakfast over we settled into groups to talk over past events and what was likely to happen in the near future.

About 10am in came a Sergeant and called out six names and took the men away along a corridor. Why, we had no idea, as they never came back that way, so we just had to sit and await our turn.

It didn't come that day and the suspense was beginning to tell its tale, because we imagined all kinds of gruesome things happening to our pals.

Eventually night came upon us once more, and another good, but worrying night in our place.

Thursday 6th June 1918

Today came round in just the same manner as before and after breakfast the same routine commenced again. Fred's name came with the first list of names, so with a solemn so long, he went away with feelings of regret.

I myself was in the next batch and after being ushered along the corridor found myself in a room like a bandstand but not open at the sides, it was surrounded by numerous doors and there I was left alone looking like a lost sheep, wondering in which direction to go.

Suddenly one of these doors opened and out came a head with a face like nothing on earth, the eyes bulging out of their sockets and a nose that looked as if it had been pickled in Schnapps for six months. I was requested to come in, so I slipped into a small cubicle like room containing a desk, two chairs and a cabinet used for filing documents, the walls were covered with vicious pictures depicting vile suggestions.

My red nosed interrogator greeted me with a very pleasant "Good morning Sergeant" and looking out of the window remarked "What a pity to be shut up on a beautiful day like this." "Yes" I said "but it could not be avoided."

"Oh yes" he said "but with a little discretion, you may have a great deal more freedom than you anticipate."

"And how am I to attain this" I asked rather doubtful of his statement.

He answered with a question "What are those red tabs on your shoulder for?"

"Some silly decorations." I answered.

"Do you smoke? Most English soldiers do I know." Handing me a small box of gold tipped cigarettes, I accepted one and thanking him very much, he struck a match, handed me a light first.

Then started the investigation in real good style and all the while my eyes were roving about this small room taking in every detail, and as to what was lying on his desk.

"How long have you been in German hands? he asked.

"Eleven days" I answered at once.

"You have had it pretty rough since you were taken, long marches, very little to eat, less to drink also no smokes"

"Quite right" I said.

"Where were you taken and on what date?"

"I was taken on the Chemis des Dames on 27th May."

"Very good" he said.

"Have you been out in France very long, and what were things like in England before you came out to join your regiment?"

"Well I was home on leave in February"

"Oh! Then you must have been out a good while because your authorities only give you leave when you have been out about twelve months I am told."

I did not answer because I knew I was letting my tongue run riot a little too far.

His next question staggered me a little and I hardly knew what to say.

"By the way what was the name of your Brigade commander?"

"I don't know." I managed to gasp out. It was not until this that I realized what I was up against.

"You don't know?" he exclaimed with some surprise.

"Well you see, he was a new one." I remarked, although the fact was that we had had ours for a while.

"Who was your divisional commander?"

"I don't know."

Sgt. Thomas William Chisholm

"Do you know the name of your Corp Commander?"

"No I don't."

"What was your Colonels name?"

"I could not say." I said looking very sheepish I should imagine.

"You don't seem to be very intelligent to hold the rank of Sergeant." He remarked with a certain amount of scorn.

"We don't need brains in the British Army to be a Sergeant, all that they want is guts, and I passed.

"Well do you know what this man on our part has cost your side?"

"What." I asked.

"Something like twenty thousand men, fifteen hundred machine guns, field guns, heavy artillery and huge dumps containing stores of food and munitions which will be very useful to our troops. Of course I am not saying we are hard pressed for food or anything like that, for instance I could go out to a restaurant in Darmstadt and order steak and chips, with two rounds of bread and a cup of coffee and it would only cost me something like two shilling and sixpence in your English money."

"Yes" I remarked quite casually "horse flesh." And with that he nearly went mad.

However when he cooled down a little I asked if I might have another cigarette, which was readily given, and we settled down once more to work.

"How did you find things in England when you were on leave? In February did you say?"

"Things were just normal" I said "There seemed to be plenty of everything that was necessary."

"Did you get plenty of food in the front line?"

"Yes, in fact the very morning I was unfortunate enough to be taken by your men, we had porridge with sugar and cows milk, followed by a good supply of bacon and tea with white bread, and no man needs more than that to fight on." I said.

"But before we go on any further, I will strike a bargain with you." I said.

"And what is that?" he said surprised.

"If you read me what is written on those two sheets of paper under your hand, I will tell you whether you are right or wrong."

"Do you understand German?" he asked.

"No" I said, "but I see some drawings on them that make me suspicious."

So he proceeded to read off one line after another, and he already had all the information he required, but I suppose he wanted it confirmed, or to add some more to it, but it was all correct and I told him so and at the same time enquiring, as to who gave him the

52

information. He remarked that they took care of people who gave them what they required.

After this my red nosed friend seemed to be fed up with his task, so pressing a bell push at his side, he said "I don't think that I need you any more today. We may meet again later." At this there entered an escort to guide me to new quarters, which were not half as comfortable my previous ones. However, there was Fred to meet me at the door, and greeting me with a smile, I was informed that he had claimed a bunk for me beside his.

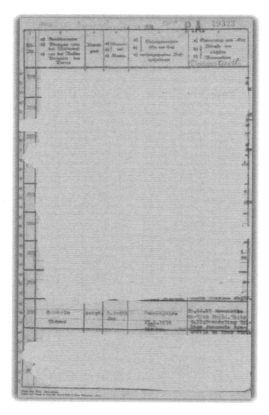

This is the Registration Document eventually completed, resulting from the Sergeants "Red Nosed Friends" notes on his arrival at Darmstadt.

Chapter 6

Work Party's etc.

Thursday 6th June 1918 to App 20th June 1917

Huts were built close together and were fitted out with wooden bunks of two tiers to accommodate four to six men, however the hut that I happened to be put into was already overcrowded, and men were crammed between the bunks on the floor, even some were underneath to get out of the way. In the centre was a large cooking range similar to those used in large houses, but it was of little use, as to a lack of fuel, it could not be used, except when it was possible to get some old packing cases, but even they were almost impossible to get.

By this time it was nearly noon and the rest of the prisoners were preparing for the midday meal, which was already on its way to our compound. We were quickly issued with small wash bowls, with which we had to do everything in, wash & shave ourselves, cook in, and eat out of, so we were not hampered with a lot of kit.

We eventually lined up with the rest to draw soup which was made up of Barley, very small portion, ground maze, Prunes, small quantity of salt fish, and the remainder water. The absence of any fats was very noticeable. All this was sent up in a large churn like tub and issued out by one of the pastors. Being almost famished it was soon put out of sight and we looked hungrily for more, but it was not available, so Fred and I retired to our hut to see if anything could be obtained there.

This went on for a good few days with monotonous regularity.

We being full ranks were not allowed on any working parties or outside the camp area, so life soon became miserable, with nothing to do but wonder about the camp from one hut to another asking for food of any kind from the more fortunate British, who were in receipt of British Red Cross parcels, but even they could ill afford to give anything away.

About this time, something like six or seven days after arriving at this camp in Darmstadt, the day being Tuesday, there seemed to be an unusual stir right through the camp. After breakfast all the British were paraded and marched away through the French and Serbian quarters and arrived at a large hut, round about which, were crowded all nationalities. We were ordered to strip to the waist and fall in with the rest.

Fred and I divested ourselves of our shirts and lined up in the slowly moving single line, behind a couple of Russians, and also behind us came a few French and

Italians. After waiting like this for about two hours we slowly got inside one door of the hut, which was divided into compartments, the one we were already in, and the next one in which we could see a German doctor and his four orderlies working very hard indeed. We were going to be inoculated. Having had some of this before, the idea did not appeal to us at all, but there was no escape, it had to be gone through. Another few steps and then came a French orderly with a jar in one hand and a brush in the other, down the line as quickly as he could, daubing everyone on the left breast with iodine.

Next, we went into the adjoining room where the white coated doctor and orderlies were each doing their special job. First one was heating the needles over a spirit stove, the next two were inserting the needles into and filling the syringe and passing it onto the M.O. who in turn injected the stuff, finally passing onto the last orderly, he cleaned away the spot of blood caused by the puncture and we passed out by another door into the open to dress again and go back our hut in our own time.

This treatment lasted every alternate day for a fortnight and the effects of this on our system was very slight, in fact it was a consolation to us, for we fully expected to be laid out for a few hours, similar to what we were when first it was done to us in England.

Sgt. Thomas William Chisholm

App. 21st June 1918

Today it poured with rain and Fred and I were confined to the hut, myself having peeled off my shirt was passing away the time examining the seams for what could be found and killed, when suddenly Fred leaned towards me and said that he was going up to the French section and told me to stay where I was until he returned. About fifteen minutes or twenty later he arrived back in his shirt sleeves carrying a small parcel. "What's happened Fred." I said. "I've flogged my jacket for this tea and sugar and small bit of bread. Get some water Bill, and let's have a feed."

I sat still with tears streaming down my face, what a pal to have I thought, to barter his very jacket for food and then come in and offer to share it with me, here was true British spirit.

Fred noticed my discomfort and rounded on me at once "Come on for God's sake, don't just sit there blubbering like a kid, get some water and let's make some tea, I'm dying for the taste of it again."

So I got some water and with dried grass and some scrap paper it boiled and Fred shared out the bread and we ate and seemed satisfied for the while.

I thought to myself, this cannot go on for long so I suggested to him with regard to my gold signet ring which had been a present to me before I left England.

Next morning we both sauntered forth to bargain once more with the French, and succeeded in getting a little more this time, in addition to the above we got about a pound of rice and a small piece of fat bacon. Delighted with this we returned to the hut and had another good feed, having enough left for the next day, which had to be stored underneath our pillows in case it was stolen.

This continued until we hardly had any personal belongings left at all. Fred had managed to get hold of a paper jacket made by the Germans from twisted paper and woven into something resembling canvas but it served its purpose very well. Finally I was without my ring, fountain pen, boots, socks cap, jacket, and various other small objects which were treasured, but had to go for food.

23rd June 1918

Today we were given our first Field Post Cards thus enabling us to write home and inform our people what had happened to us and where we were. The card itself was not for use by British prisoners but the French, who were superior in numbers by about twenty to one, however it served its purpose. We could not say very much owing to it having to be censored, and the chances of giving any information away, so all that could be written was to the effect of, in good health, safe and hoping all was well at home. This card was handed in for dispatch on the same as it was issued. *(An after note said it reached England 30th July 1918.)*

Sgt. Thomas William Chisholm

His card follows, and he wrote:

My Dear Mother, Just a line to let you know that I am keeping well at present hoping all at home are the same. I am able to write to you once a month, I thought you would perhaps like to hear from me when I am in my present state as a prisoner but one point is I am finished with the war and am sure of a safe return all at present. I Remain You Loving Son, Will.

Sgt. Thomas William Chisholm

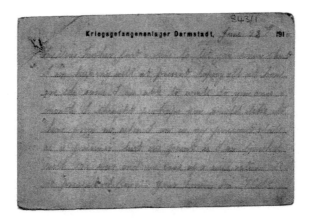

There has been a special order issued by the camp commandant that in future British troops in captivity would salute German N.C.O's from the rank of corporal upwards. This came as a very unpleasant shock to us and was the cause for a great buzz of excitement and indignation amongst us. It was decided to ignore the order, as we were all of the same frame of mind and if we all carried out our intentions it would not be possible for them to put us all in cells at once. It was carried out very well indeed, for if we noticed an N.C.O. (non commissioned officer) coming at all we were always looking the other way, or would dodge round the corner of one of the huts which happened to be nearest, thus we always robbed Gerry of his looked for salute.

Chapter 7

Cattle Trucks, & Three Days to Lamsdorf

Monday 1st July 1918

Orders came today that we were going to move and while handing in blankets, I was accosted by my old red nosed friend, who with a smile, approached and asked how I had enjoyed my stay at Darmstadt. Not to be outdone I replied that it had all been very nice, only I saw that he had noticed my plight, being without boots etc, and drawing me to one side he asked if at any time during my tour of the front I had met any regiment of the Canadian Scottish. The truth was that I had not and said so rather indignantly and I could see that the swine did not believe me, however after that I saw no more of him and by 2pm we were aboard the train made up of about twenty cattle trucks and rolled away.

The journey lasted 3 days and was not without it's outstanding events. There were 35 men in one truck. The first day we travelled from 2pm until somewhere about 3:30am 2nd July before we got a meal at all, as after various stops for such as coal, water and perhaps a new engine driver. All we could do was look through the little opening in the top of the truck between iron bars. The place began to smell owing to so many men being in the confined space and no sanitary arrangements. There were neither blankets, or straw to lie upon and I fully expected someone to go mad before the journey was over.

It was a great relief to get outside that truck, although it was so early in the morning and bitterly cold, we gladly lined up in the canteen on the station for a meal consisting of something like macaroni. The amount seemed very small indeed to our starved insides, but the main thing about it was it was hot. As soon as we had eaten this we were driven back by our guards to the trucks and away again.

Daylight at last and on looking through the lattice, found that we were traveling along the Rhine valley, and a beautiful sight it was with the pine clad hills coming right down to the waters edge. Nearly all the hill tops were crowned with what appeared to be baronial castles standing out against the skyline and in the hollows nestled the beautiful hamlets or villages. However, on we rolled with the sweet smelling pine trees in our nostrils mingling with the stench of the truck.

About midday we came to a halt beside a small village, the children were just coming out of school. Seeing the train with prisoners aboard and being curious as all children will be, they made a line straight for the train and getting as close as they could began to

throw stones and making the motion of cutting out throats. Of course we were helpless and naturally annoyed that children so young should be taught to do such things, but there it was, proving their utter hatred of the British. After about half an hour we puffed away once more and continued until 9pm before another halt was called, this time at a station, fairly large with a canteen on the platform, another meal similar to the last, then once more aboard and away again, still keeping along the Rhine Valley.

Wednesday 3rd July 1918

At about 10am this morning we arrived at a small station called Lamsdorf, where we were finally doomed to settle for the duration of the war. After the usual formalities had been gone through, we moved off in the direction of the camp, which proved to be a very big one indeed.

Except for a few scattered houses here and there, the place seemed to be devoid of any civilization, the inhabitants being mainly German troops and a good lot of Uhlans (Light Cavalry men) were passed, who grinned with satisfaction at the sight of us and no wonder, the plight of us, unwashed and unshaven for days, we had a most unkempt appearance. However we trudged on, grumbling all the way not knowing what was to become of us, and when we were going to get something to eat. On through the encampment into open country and about half a mile away was what was called Lager 3A, which we made for, with two British guides in attendance from Lager 1.

We arrived at the large barbed wire gates, and from the inside, came the Camp Commandant with his usual followers and we were duly handed over to his care. After being counted and the roll called we were split into parties of fifty and marched through two high walls of wire about 12 feet high and 6 feet apart.

All round the camp, just outside the outside the outer belt of barbed wire, was a shallow trench, the earth having been banked up behind to form the beat for our main guards, who patrolled night and day, two sentries meeting at a certain point, and immediately behind this miniature embankment, and also at the corner of the camp, was the big hut which housed the whole guard when off duty. About 20 yards to the right of this hut was a high wooden erection with a square covered in platform, this at times was being manned by a section of machine gunners.

It happened that the place allotted to us was at the very end of the camp, right up close to the North Eastern edge of the Black Forest. The camp or part was divided into three compounds, each containing six huts, 1 larger hut was to be used as a wash house, also furnished with a large pump with two handles to it. The huts faced the dense forest in two lines of three. The one Fred and I were put into was in the rear and centre. They were about 80 feet long, 10 feet wide by 8 feet high, lighted by two windows, with a double door in the centre above which was fitted one electric light just inside the door. About 2 feet of the building was above ground, the rest having been sunk into the ground, so we had to descend earthen steps to enter. The beds were built of pitch pine in groups of four, with a board placed on edge to separate each mans bed from the other. Having staked our claim near the door and also the one and only large combustion store, we sallied forth to draw blankets, and wash bowls. Each man was given two blankets, which must have seen service in the wars of 1870, judging by their condition. However they were better than nothing at all.

After this we were roused out again by huts or barracks and counted by our guards and a little Sergeant Major. When this was done, a meal was supplied made up of barley, ground maize, prunes, salt fish and water, the latter being very much in evidence.

That done the senior in each barrack was given orders through an interpreter to make out a list of men under him, with duties for each day, such as working parties, men to go to the cook house to bring in the soup for each meal, then our first day's work was done and about 9pm everyone was in or on his boards and asleep.

Thus ended Thursday 3rd July and our first day at our new home.

Chapter 8

Lamsdorf Our New Home From Hell

Friday 4th July 1918

Now it was just, settle down and make yourselves as comfortable as you can, because dear knows how long you are likely to be here.

This morning our guards started straight away with working parties, ever one was made to fall in on parade after a meal at 5.30 am and following the usual count, the Sergeants were allowed to stay in the camp and the remainder, some 200 men being split up into equal parties and placed under special guard, were marched off to their various duties. Some were taken down to Lamsdorf station, to unload trucks, others to the cook house, some to the hospital to bury the dead, others were taken into the forest to cut wood.

These duties went on with monotonous regularity for about 8 or 10 weeks, the same thing day after day. Three meals of soup and working parties, until, while talking one night amongst ourselves, someone suggest that we should form a committee with the view to organizing some kind of sports or concert parties and it was decided to do this. The committee were elected, and started work right away, but everything seemed to be against us, because whether from fear of any attempted escapes, or sheer cussedness our Lager Commandant refused to recognize the committee.

Not to be out done, next day whilst on working party at the rail head with number one Lager, the members of the committee, had a conversation with our commander in that area, and it was decided that he would serve on the committee along with us, because it was thought that together they might have a little more chance of a hearing with the Commandant, but still this failed.

Still this did not make us lose heart, and at night in the huts after all work had finished, we used to hold impromptu concerts, the artists being made up of men from all over England, Scotland and Wales. We had five men from Wales with beautiful voices, so their help was enlisted, along with a comedian from Liverpool, one from Scotland, and one man from Durham used to sing and recite all our Tyneside stuff, so we were not lacking in talent. This went on for a good while, and the practice gave all the necessary confidence, when we did get the chance of a decent show.

Sgt. Thomas William Chisholm

Wednesday 14th August 1918

Today at 2pm we were roused from our after dinner siesta by our guards, absolutely chased out on parade and ordered to take with us all blankets and clothing in our possession and were marched across to Lager 1 for a bath. We were very happy at the thought of a good old splash to relieve us of some of the dirt and lice.

First we entered what appeared to be a boiler house, but it proved to contain large fumigating appliances. We were made to strip naked, and put every article into our blankets with a tally, on which was written regiment, rank, and number, and in we went a dozen at a time.

From there we went along a corridor into a large room containing six chairs, which turned out to be used as barber chairs. While six of the first twelve were seated, the others were handed a pair of hair cutting shears and were made, under supervision, to literally shave off all the hair of the others. We did look like real prisoners after this operation, and of course when the first six had been done the squads changed over.

With the first twelve finished, we were called to the corner of the room, where one of the Germans also had a chair and a small table. On it was an enamel bowl containing a quantity of what appeared to be clay of a light bluish colour. Motioning me to mount the chair and stand with my feet apart, my attendant mixed up the mixture with a thin flat piece of wood, then using the piece of wood he plastered the mixture on all parts of my body where a growth of hair appeared. That done, and with a mumbled request to "Rouse" I was sent out into the corridor in the direction of the shower bath to await my turn to enter.

The conversations centred on the subject as to what it was that had been applied to our nether organs. Some said soap, others suggested a special kind of ointment used in special cases, but eventually we were all wrong.

It had the most vile smell, but during the talking and waiting, one man in particular had spread the stuff as far over his body as it would go, in the expectation of a nice lather when it came to his time to get under the shower. In doing so he had unthinkingly scratched his eye owing to some irritation. He happened to be just in front of me when it came to his time to enter the shower/bath and the water had been turned on.

Try to picture our faces when we observed his eyebrows slowly beginning to move down his face. The more water he applied, the more the hair came away. When at last the toilet had been finished, there was not a vistage of hair left on our bodies. We were as bare as the day we were born.

Then of course it was time to hear some real soldiers language, and we did hear it, between fits of laughter from those who seemed to see the funny side of it, but it was unanimously decided that this was the first and last occasion on which our caretakers would entice us out for a bath.

Sgt. Thomas William Chisholm

Although not noted in his diary, the Sergeant sent a postcard 25th August 1918 on which he wrote:

> *My Dear Mother, Just a few lines when I have the opportunity. I think it is about two months ago since I last wrote to you, but since then nothing of importance has happened, only my address has changed. I am still keeping well at present hoping you are the same at home. I have not got my Red Cross Parcels yet, but hope to do so soon, and when I get them I will manage along quite alright, I only wish this war was all over, however I don't suppose it will last very long now. Well mother you can write to this address safely so I will have to close for the present. Hoping to hear from you soon. I Remain, Your Loving Son, Will*
> *xxxxxxx*

The card was dekivered 26th Novermber 1918.

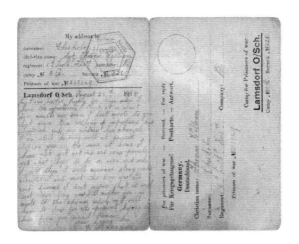

Sgt. Thomas William Chisholm

Friday 27th September 1918

All this time as prisoners there had never been any sign of a parcel from England, and we had been told that after about twelve weeks we would be in receipt of parcels of food and clothing from the British Red Cross Society.

However today we all got a pleasant surprise. While the men were at their various tasks, Fred and I were searching round from one compound to another trying to get something to eat, when we spied one of the members of the committee from Lager One coming across towards our camp and trying to catch our attention. When near enough he called out that he wanted to speak to us, so we made for the main gate to wait for him.

He told us that a whole consignment of emergency packets had arrived from the International Headquarters of the YMCA in Berlin to be distributed amongst us and it would be one packet per man. So, delighted with the news we speedily told the remainder of the men in our camp and I might say it caused some excitement.

When the boys returned from work they told us that they had actually handled the packets and some of the men had been kept back to bring them across to us from Lager One. They arrived about 2pm and were quickly issued. Eager to see what they contained, instead of going into the hut we sat down in the open and fairly tore off the wrappers. Lo and behold, what a sight for sore eyes, it was as if a miracle had been performed. I think there was a lump in everybody's throat and tears of joy in their eyes, the contents was:

2 x 1lb packets of Huntley & Palmers Biscuits
3   Tins of Bully Beef
2   Tins of Cheese
1   Tin of Dripping
2   Tins of Milk
1   Tin of Cocoa
1 x 1/4lb of Tea
5   Packets of Woodbines
1 x 1lb Bar of Pale Soap
1 x 1/4lb Tobacco
1 x 1/4lb of Oats
1 x 1/2lb of Sugar

We were so anxious and hungry that it was impossible to decide what to eat first, however Fred came to the rescue. He was going to have a dish of Porridge first, then some real Tea with biscuits spread with dripping. It was decided that Fred being the cook, he should make the meal. Meanwhile we were all smoking furiously, not having had a real smoke for such a long time.

What a feast it was, sitting on the floor of that dirty whitewashed hut with our homemade tin cups and wash bowls, it just was the finest meal that we had ever had in our lives.

That done I filled my pipe, and washed up all the dishes, ready for the next feed which came at 9pm.

The cabbage soup that was sent by the cookhouse for our tea, was sent back as it came, we firmly refused to touch it. Gerry was rather annoyed about it, but I am certain that we got the same soup three days later, after our parcels had been devoured.

Saturday 28th September 1918

By this time, our guards were becoming very friendly towards us, owing to the fact that they had less trouble with our boys, and also they were much better workers than the other nationalities. At night after work was over, some of them would come into our huts and talk to us about the war and its effects on different countries.

We soon learned in this way that Germany itself was about the worst off, as quite confidentially they told us that real tea was almost unobtainable, and if they could get it they had to pay 40 marks per pound, bread also 40 marks and soup 42 marks.

The tea that we used to get was made from Bay leaves dried, then scalded in the usual way. We were allowed 2 ozs of meat per week, but this was horseflesh, black and evil smelling, so it was usually thrown away or given to the Russians, who came round our compound after every meal to see if there was anything leftover.

Instead of drinking their tea, Fred and I would dig up some dandelion roots, wash them very clean, cut them up into very small pieces, roast them on a piece of tin until they were black, then boiled them until the water was coloured. This was found to be a good medicine, so it was adopted throughout the camp.

When the guards discovered we were in possession of such a large quantity of soap from our parcels, they became even more friendly, in the hope of getting small pieces for their own personal use. We eventually bartered with them one day and it was arranged that at between 10 and 12 midnight Fred would crawl across to the outer belt of barbed wire, pass through the soap, and in return he would get a sandbag full of potatoes. Of course the ordinary sandbag would hold nearly two and a half stones of potatoes and was considered a very good prize indeed. This exchange went on for a couple of nights when we found that if we did not economize, our supply of soap would soon be exhausted. Fred and I put our heads together and arranged a little joke on Gerry. Getting a small portion of clay, and shaping it to appear as if it was a piece of soap that had been used, we then proceeded to give it a thin coating of soap, and after having washed our hands it appeared to be a perfectly nice large portion. This was made our last exchange and we bargained for a double amount of potatoes. After this we had to make ourselves scarce and blend into the background.

Meanwhile the concert party are making great strides.

Sgt. Thomas William Chisholm

Sunday 29th September 1918

Out on parade at 8.15 am, we were marched out of the camp to our first church service. We arrived at some cavalry barracks, where, in a large stable an alter had been temporarily fixed up. The priest in charge being German, could speak English pretty well and he was assisted by two volunteers from the British section, but what a motley crowd it was. Crammed into that stable were British, French, Italian, Russians, Bulgarians, Romanians, Serbs and Germans. The service seemed to be drawn out at length and we men were not sorry when it was all over and we managed to get a breath of fresh air and move.

After church, we were back into the compound again with nothing to do but lounge about, it was torture, we all seemed so cramped. About 11.30am Fred and I were walking round, hands behind our backs, when we were approached by a very tall man wearing a long cloak and a parsons flat hat. He came straight towards us with the greeting "Good morning Englishman. It is very cold today yes no" "Good morning sir" we answered "It is cold". Then followed the usual talk about the state of affairs and putting our trust in God to put things right when he thought fit.

Having passed on, we continued up the roadway until reaching the compound gates. Fred suddenly suggested making some pies with the remainder of our biscuits and bully beef, so we set off back again to set about it straight away. I lit a fire out in the open and built a small oven with a piece of tin and some clay. This done I left it to dry, while selecting 6 or 8 good potatoes and proceeded to clean and boil them.

Meanwhile Fred was busy in the hut grating down the last of our biscuits to a fine powder, I might mention here that not being in possession of the usual nutmeg grater we manufactured one from a piece of tin about 6 inches square and perforated all over with very small nail holes, this was a very useful article indeed. So with the cooked potatoes, mashed into a pulp, they were mixed with the powered biscuits and a little milk to a paste. Our pie tins were made from some old cheese tins, being about four and a half inches in diameter and half an inch deep with the rough edges hammered down, and these were lined with the paste. Next was added the bully beef, with a slice of two of potatoes on top, then sprinkled with salt. Finally the crust was put on top, and up into the improvised oven and cooked by Fred himself.

Just as he was ready to go out, it commenced to snow, but not to be daunted Fred sat throughout that awful blizzard until his pies were nice and brown. He had the very devil's luck, with the wet snow running down at the back of the hole and he had to keep blowing the fire with his mouth nearly all of the time. I felt really sorry for him but he wouldn't allow me to relieve him.

Having eaten these pies, followed by a drink of good strong tea, it was announced that the sub-committee were to have a meeting with the Lager One Committee, with a view to getting a show put on, but this application was unsuccessful.

Monday 30th September 1918

After the snowstorm of yesterday the air was crisp and clear and as usual following the breakfast at 4:45am the various working parties were sent about their tasks. One of the boys next to where I lay was rather ill so I suggested that we exchange jackets, which would enable him to have a day's rest, and I could go out to work for him for a change and see if it was possible to get food of any kind. I was doomed to disappointment, as I was put into the last party to leave camp and we arrived at the forest to collect wood for use in the camp.

We left the camp pulling a large wagon with very high sloping sides, and penetrated for about two and a half miles into the dense Black Forest. The work was slow and laborious, owing to the absence of any definite roadway, we just had to thread our way through the high pine trees wherever it was possible to get the wagon through. At last our guards called a halt, and set us about our work gathering loose pieces of wood and loading the wagon. Meanwhile the guards filled their long pipes with loose leaves, and smoked them, watching us all the time.

After working like this for half an hour along came a Gerry gamekeeper, dressed in a green trilby hat tilted up at one side, with a coloured feather stuck in, green jacket and riding breeches, leggings, and carrying a gun across his arm. He spotted one of our men breaking a large branch off a tree, and by heaven he did go off the deep end. He cursed everyone who came near him and when he did cool down and went on his way our guards said something about him, which I think was not very complimentary. In fact one became so annoyed that he lifted up his rifle by the muzzle and his actions suggested that he was about to smash it over the wagon wheel, had not one of his comrades not called him to order in time.

Another half hour work and we were bound back for camp with a good heavy load of timber, which took longer to haul back than it took to come out, but we got back in time for our soup dinner.

All seemed well with no work in the afternoon, which I was thankful for, for I was dog tired, and in need of rest, because it was the first day's work I had done since I had been taken, and a good sleep was had that night.

Chapter 9

October, Another Month, and Rumours of Peace Talks.

Tuesday 1st October 1918

Today started just as many others have started with the usual breakfast and working parties.

News reaches us that the civil population is to be allowed another rise in their bread ration of 10%.

When the boys return after work it is with rumours of terms of peace by President Wilson, also that the railway workers in Austria had gone on strike owing to some misunderstanding, and that they were refusing to convey German troops across their country.

Wednesday 2nd October 1918

Today Fred and I agree to adopt a young lad belonging to Durham, who was serving in the West Yorkshire regiment at the time he was taken, so young Billy is taken under our wing.

The first biscuit parcel is delivered to us, so to celebrate both events Fred makes us some potato cakes, and with a pot of tea and the biscuits the feed goes down very well.

The task of ridding ourselves of superfluous hair, of which there was ample growth, was no easy one. No one was in possession of the necessary razor, brush or soap, so it had been impossible to shave up to the present, and now after a whole month we felt the need of one badly. Fred spotted one of the boys with a small pair of nail scissors, so asking for the loan of them he placed himself in front of a piece of polished tin and proceeded to clip off his beard. After about an hour and a half he gave up, so I volunteered to complete the job. We adjourned outside into the open compound and I started to snip, snip, snip. Judging by the length of time it took, I must have only snipped one hair at a time, for I kept going for another two hours, but at the end of that time, Fred looked a great deal cleaner than before, and he in turn clipped mine, which took just as long. Eventually it became the daily spare time pastime of all in the camp as it proved better than nothing at all, although we could not get the hair completely removed, for a rough stubble remained, it was good enough for the time being.

Thursday 3rd October 1918

We have reported to us that the treatment of British POW's in the mines is most brutal, they are being forced to go down the coal mine without any food, with orders that they would have to produce a certain amount of coal before they would be allowed to come to the surface again. Of course through lack of nourishment and ill treatment, the men were in no fit condition to work, so they were obliged to remain below for many days at a time and never seeing daylight. If they were unfortunate enough to suffer any accident, they had to carry on just the same, without any dressing on their wounds, through which many of them had died. Cases arrived in our camp one day, and two or three of them were Romanians. They had been returned from the salt mines in some unknown district, but they had been kept down the mines so long, that they were totally blind. Whether they would ever regain their sight at all was never bothered about.

Sgt. Thomas William Chisholm

Friday 4th October 1918

Good things happen today when the boys come back from work, they also bring news of emergency parcels. Not being sufficient to give one to every man, they are opened out and the goods pooled and then issued out. Our share consists of one and a half kilos of bread biscuits and 4 Gerry soup powders per man. With the three lots of rations together, the next few days looked a bit better.

Saturday 5th October 1918

We were so hungry last night that all our biscuits have been consumed, three or four times during the night Fred and I would wake up and speaking in low tones would make up our minds that the these two biscuits would be the last. Of course Billy was in on it as well, but after dosing for about another two hours, our resolution would be broken, and we would have another couple, thus when morning came round we had none left at all, and we were waiting for our ration of black bread.

Billy got his first clothing parcel from the Red Cross, so he straight away stripped off all his old clothing and having a bath in cold water, dressed up in his new outfit he looks very well indeed.

A rumour comes again into the camp, this time it is reported that the King of Bulgaria has disappeared, but this is all we ever hear of it.

Sunday 6th October 1918

This morning we are all punished for some reason, by the camp commandant depriving us of our breakfast soup and we only get our bread ration, so we have to be content with that. We cut ours in halves and spread it over with a layer of very course salt, and gathering a few dandelion leaves, we eat this and have to be satisfied. Unfortunately, owing to there being so few British officers in the camp, our complaints never get a hearing.

Off to the usual Sunday church parade and then lounging about for the rest of the day, then our pastor issues postcards to us so we pass away a little of the time writing home.

This postcard reaches England 26th November 1918, and on it he wrote:

My Dear Mother, Just a few lines to let you know that I am still keeping well at present, hoping all at home are the same. I am not doing bad at all as my parcels have started coming through and the food they contain is very good indeed, thanks to the Red Cross. I am still waiting of a letter from you to hear how everyone is keeping at home. I am sorry to say that I am unable to write letters as they have been stopped, or I

would be able to write more. However we may get the privilege again
sooner or later. Until then I'm afraid I will have to draw to a close so
Goodbye for present. I Remain, Your Loving Son Will xxxxxxxxx

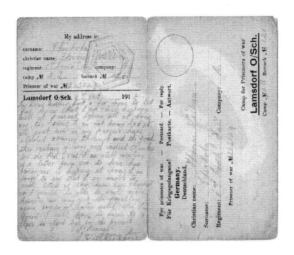

In the afternoon, Fred, Billy and myself wander
away through the camp amongst the other nationalities
in the hope of getting something. But everything we do
seems so hopeless.

At one part of the camp where the Serbians are, we
come across some of these people struggling with huge
packing cases absolutely filled with bacon, the sight of
which nearly sent us mad. To cap it all, it has been sent
from British Red Cross people in Switzerland. We

wished we had not come so far now. It was suggested that we should make a raid on their compound and steal what we could at night, but if that had been attempted there would certainly be some shooting on the part of our sentries, and very stern punishments next morning so it was called off. So we did without again.

Monday 7th October 1918

News comes through that the peace terms submitted by President Wilson have been almost accepted by the Germans, with certain modifications.

This afternoon our pasterns approach the compound in mass formation with rifles and bayonets fixed. On their arrival the Dalmatian (our translator) is called, to inform us that we are to proceed again for another visit to the baths. On hearing this of course it is greeted with very strong dissent, and we refuse to go. Gerry not to be daunted, endeavours to rouse us out, but as soon as the men left the huts they scattered in all directions, thus making it impossible to get us all together. Fred, Billy and I disappeared into the French settlement, and from the top of the huts watched the proceedings from there. We could see both British and German all over the place, the Germans shouting and waving their arms about in an endeavour to call us all in, but it could not be done. In the end the senior Corporal must have reported the matter to his Commandant, and finally they were withdrawn, and we gradually arrived back to the huts in small numbers.

It was on our arrival that we found out all that had happened. It appeared that one pastern had entered number 124 barrack and attempted to rouse out all who remained inside, but he came to grief because, losing his temper at being ignored by so many men, he had unfixed his bayonet, and stamping along towards a Corporal of the 6th Battalion Northumberland Fusiliers, was just in the act of crashing the flat of the bayonet across his shoulder, when there was a yell of rage and pain from Gerry. He had obtained the full contents of a pot containing steaming hot cocoa in his face. Being in such a rage he had failed to observe a mirror just in front of the Corporal, placed at such an angle, that whilst standing with his back to Gerry, he could still see all that was going on behind him, so when Gerry was about to strike him, the Corporal got in first, with a quick movement of his arm across his shoulder, just managed to hit his mark, and Gerry got the contents full in the face.

The Corporal was put straight under arrest, and put into cells until next morning when he was brought up before the camp Kommandant. In the meantime we had all been very busy gathering together all the evidence of the assault we could and sent five men as witnesses for the defense. After a trial lasting half an hour, it ended that instead of our good Corporal being punished, the boot was on the other foot, and Gerry was put in cells for six days and then sent back to his regiment at the front.

That also ended any more attempts on Gerry's part to get us to go for a bath, because we did not want a repetition of our last bath, and fumigation.

Sgt. Thomas William Chisholm

Tuesday 8th October 1918

The report of yesterday is confirmed by our committee men from Lager 1 when we all met today to receive an Emergency Parcel between two, and then we have another blow out.

It is customary everyday to see our Russian neighbours moving in and out of the various compounds, selling or exchanging cigarettes for bread. The method used was for one portion of bread, you can obtain five cigarettes which after all are equal to two and a half Woodbines, because they were half cardboard holder and the other half tobacco, so we called then half and halves. Otherwise you could purchase them at five for one mark, but not being in possession of any money at all, we are forced to give our daily bread ration away if we want a smoke. This has been going on for a while now and we're just about tired of doing without the only piece of solid food that we could get, in fact I think that a few of the boys were on the border of madness.

However this morning it was a strange Russian who came around with his box of smokes and he shuffled his six foot six of solid manhood across to where a group of Tommies were standing muttering, "Cigarettes, homemade ugaritten! for marks?". So an NCO who formerly was a dock labourer at Liverpool and a proper ruffian, moved forward to meet him saying "Rusky here come", and started to bargain with him, but the Russian seemed a little doubtful whether to accept the bread or not, but at last he was persuaded and the Sergeant started to select his own cigarettes from the box with the remainder of the guys looking on. Suddenly, without any warning, the whole box went flying into the air, with the cigarettes scattering in all directions. Naturally when the Russian fully realized what had happened he tried to collect as many as he could, but some of the men beat him to it and disappeared into the huts with what they could. I fully expected to see him fly into a rage and charge into the crowd like a mad bull, (because he seemed big enough to eat all our men, and look for more), but instead he just said "Ah, homemade mine cigaretten, dat is nix goot" and the tears streamed down his dirty face. Fancy, he a big hulking brute of a man actually crying at the loss of a few cigarettes, however he had to go away without any of them, for the gang had stolen nearly the whole lot.

The excitement died down and they were all being smoked, when about half an hour later up came another Russian who happened to be in charge of his own countrymen, and a Sergeant Major. He greeted the few who were standing about with a pleasant "Good morning Englishmen" and we returned to the compound. Coming up close to the wire he asked who it was who had stolen his comrade's cigarettes. Being what we were I suppose, no one answered, because the real culprit was hiding in his hut and even though I and the few who were present had taken no part whatever in the proceedings, we did not wish to be implicated by trying to defend one who could lower his dignity as an English NCO.

"Well" he said "I am very surprised at your actions this morning, fancy an Englishman coming so low, as to steal such a trifle from my people, because they knew you preferred a smoke to your bread. You know my people are not educated as you are, and are not to be expected to know so much as you, and I know very well that you would never dream of doing such a cowardly act in your own country, because I was educated in Oxford University, and I know your ways.

At this we fairly gasped in astonishment, at the very idea of the man in front of us standing stiffly to attention in his smart Russian uniform, his peaked cap, and blouse, smartly cut riding britches and last but not least a very smart pair of boots, high legged, such as worn by all Russians and polished as I have never seen any boots before.

However he apologized very properly for the intrusion and said that he hoped that we would think twice before doing anything like that again, and went

away leaving us feeling very small and humiliated indeed.

Three days later the same gentleman, under the pretext of going to a church service in the neighbouring village, escaped in the horse and trap that were being used to convey him there, and he was never seen again.

Sgt. Thomas William Chisholm

Wednesday 9th October 1918

Today opened very unsatisfactorily owing to a North East wind blowing and rain coming down in sheets. All working parties are cancelled, and the sentries seek shelter wherever they can.

The barracks or huts became flooded, with the absence of any scheme of drainage. The water poured through the roofs of the huts onto nearly all the beds and we are all sitting shivering in groups where ever there is a dry spot to be found. Our pastern has great difficulty in getting any one to venture across to the cook house to bring the soup, but after a great deal of noise he gets his way at last.

There is no sleep tonight on account of the storm and the rain coming in on our beds.

Thursday 10th October 1918

Cheerful news greets us this morning about 10.30am, when a messenger from Lager One gave the information that a truck load of biscuits was lying at the station and our working party was busy unloading them in readiness to be brought across to us.

This is the first biscuit parcel that I have received since I came into Germany, so it is with great joy that I took possession of my wooden box containing about 3 kilos. It was sent from Bern in Switzerland on the 9th of September, so it has taken just one month to reach me. There was a printed card enclosed, to be used for the purposes of a receipt, which I immediately filled in and returned to Bern.

It is rumoured about the camp today that a new Turkish Government is about to be formed with a Prime minister at its head who had been in England for many years and was more inclined to the side of the allies than he was to the German side. Of course we fully expected at this rate, that Turkey would eventually turn against Germany and come over to our side, but this rumour also died a natural death as we heard no more of it.

I don't feel all together too well today, what with that empty feeling in the pit of the stomach and the rotten raw cabbage soup I get it into my head that it is the end and begin to pray that it might be so. It is not only the sickly feeling, but together, the stink of the huts we are living in, and we are all absolutely walking with lice, one could not get a minutes peace for scratching one part of the body or another. Not being able to get a wash or shave we all just feel as if there was nothing more to live for, however night comes again and with it sleep, with the hope that the war would be finished soon.

Sgt. Thomas William Chisholm

Friday 11th October 1918

When daylight broke I was too ill to turn out, so Fred took it upon himself to nurse me, it was a bad attach of flu and he gave me all my food at my bunk and would not allow me out of the bed at all, although I managed to crawl out in the evening for a little while but was glad to get back again.

Saturday 12th October 1918

Both Fred and Billy get biscuit parcels today, this is the first one for Fred and he is overjoyed to think that at last someone has realized that he is still alive and in need of food.

At 10.30pm the atmosphere became so still, that it seemed impossible to breath. What was coming we had no idea, but we had not long to wait, for as we were lounging ideally about outside the huts, as it seemed a little too early to turn in, because the mere fact of having no work or exercise of any description, we naturally suffered from sleeplessness. It came upon us quite suddenly. In the distance a terrific roar could be heard and within five minutes the storm burst. Such a storm I have never experienced before and don't wish to again. The wind simply tore down upon us, so of course the best thing to do was to get under cover.

With the wind came the deafening crash of thunder. The heavens were literally one mass of liquid fire, just like a million gas jets burning here, there, and all over. The most peculiar thing about the whole affair, was that there was not one drop of rain. It just seemed as if all hell had opened. We were so, I would not say afraid, but surprised, that no one seemed as if they could speak. We just all stood round the inside of the doorway and watched, absolutely amazed that the elements could play such tricks.

Needless to say the sentries had also disappeared, into the guard hut. Once again, we could if inclined, go free, but what use in such a storm, and having to keep under cover of the forest, which we would have been forced to do, would have been courting death.

The sky seemed to have fallen so low, that it seemed as if one could touch it with an outstretched hand and the lightening, small jagged forks, thousands of them. It was never dark for one minute, a' truly nerve racking experience for one who had never been through an electric storm before.

The storm kept raging until somewhere about four or five am. Finally the gale or hurricane seemed to blow itself out, with it the thunder and lightning died away and quiet reigned once more.

It was then that we felt the need of a little rest, for not one of the troops had made any attempt at sleep, which had been out of the question. I don't think that anyone failed that night, to offer up a small prayer of some sort, for our safety.

Sunday 13th October 1918

A miserable wet day dawned and when it was time to parade and for the usual count, it was then that we saw what havoc had been done by last nights storm. One of the machine gun towers had been smashed to pieces and burnt by lightening. Great huge pine trees had been torn out of the earth by the roots and carried 50 yards away, and lay like fallen giants. Some were split from top to bottom. It was only the sight of these things that made us realize the full force of the storm, its affect on nature and we had no desire to go through the same again.

We went as usual on our tramp to the stable for church service. On our return, along came the German Sergeant Major and had us all turned out on parade again for a message from the Lager Kommandant. He thought it very silly of us British people wanting to buy a piano for our concert party. When, he thought, in all probability we would not be there very long. We informed the Sgt. Maj. that our committee would take a vote on the matter and let the Kommandant know within the hour, to which he agreed.

Finally it was decided that instead of getting the piano we might obtain permission to erect a small monument in the cemetery to our comrades who had died in captivity. This was agreed to and conveyed to the Kommandant who demurred a good deal, however in the end he informed us that he would write to Head Quarters and see what could be done.

Dinnertime arrived and it was just pigs meal, consisting of a very small percentage of Barley, potato skins, jam, died fungus from trees and their substitute for margarine. None of the ingredients having been washed, the result was about a quarter of an inch of sand and soil in the bottom of our work bowls. Needless to say, no matter how hungry we felt we could not settle to consume this, but it was soon devoured by our Russian visitors, who were continually coming round begging for what they could get.

The weather dried up somewhat towards 2pm so Fred, Billy and myself sauntered off in search of adventure. We arrived in a part of the camp where there was a piece of open ground and here we found all sorts of nationalities selling anything from a pin, to a gold watch. It was very amusing to walk round this market (for that's what it was) and view the various articles. Here you could bargain for a pair of trousers, stitched and darned where they had been worn, in exchange for a tin of bully beef and 2 biscuits. In another, a pocket knife for so many cigarettes. One particular fellow had a beautiful silver watch, wonderfully chased on the outside and mounted with 17 rubies, and it was no thicker than a 5 shilling piece. He wanted 200 marks for it, but not being in possession of any money at all, we passed on to the next stand. Here we found an Italian with about 2 dozen pieces of black bread. He was trying to sell these for 3 marks a piece, another chap half naked was exchanging Gerry soup powders for 10 cigarettes.

We spent a good two hours wandering round this market, and finally not being able to pinch anything, we returned to our compound in disgust.

Sgt. Thomas William Chisholm

Monday 14th October 1918

Up as usual at 4:45am, after breakfast we are split up into working parties, so after I borrow one of the boys jackets, and I set off with the rest of our party to work in the forest.

This time we took a different road, and after going about 2 miles our sentries called a halt, and sent us about our business. Myself and one of our party branched out in a north easterly direction and after one or two journeys back and forward to the wagon with armfuls of wood, we decided that the time was ripe to carry out our plans as arranged on our journey out. Moving away until we were absolutely hidden by the trees and the undergrowth, we moved quicker until after travelling about half a mile we came to a clearing which from all appearances looked as if it had been meant for a road but was not finished. After a good look round to see that we had not been observed, we made up towards the edge of the forest which was at the end of this road and up a slight incline, but keeping under cover all the time, because we had no fancy to be shot at for escaping. When we arrived at the top of the hill we saw that it led into a large potato field, where all the potato's had been pulled out of the earth and were just lying in small heaps as if ready to be collected.

"Whatever can we carry them in?" my pal said, "I know" said I "Just pull your shirt up like this." So pulling up our shirts blouse fashion, we crawled forward until we were close enough to one of the heaps and started to fill our improvised sacks. When we were finished I might say we looked anything but in proportion, nevertheless we thought it was time to get back in case our party had decided to go back to camp, or we had been missed. We were very lucky, because just as we were within sight of the wagon again, the sentries began calling the party in to go back. Gathering a large bundle of branches, almost more than we could carry, we spread them over our backs, and almost bent double with the weight, we were able to hide the tell tale bulk in our fronts. It was a nightmare of a journey what with the potatoes pressing and rubbing against our prominent ribs and the soil and weight, it was absolutely hell, not counting the fear of being caught by Gerry. I for one was jolly glad to be back in camp again and get myself unburdened. We had a good feed that night.

Billy, our adopted one is sent out on a party in the afternoon employed in the burial of Russians. He told us on his return that they had buried forty. The majority had died from dysentery and the smell was almost unbearable. The bodies had all been put into one grave fully clothed just as they had died.

The Unwilling Fox Terrier

During the course of the afternoon when all seemed to be quiet in the huts, Fred and I were walking alongside the outer wall of wire, close up to the sentries beat when Fred uttered a sound of amazement. On looking round I saw a small rough haired fox terrier coming in our direction. I think he must have belonged to one of the German troops stationed just across the moor, in the direction of Lager 1.

It so happened that we had never seemed to notice the fact that since being in Germany we had never seen a dog at all and this being the first, brought home to both at once, the same thought. As horrible and cruel as it may seem, hunger drives a man to any extremes. We both looked at each other and murmured "here is a feed". We intended if possible to get hold of the dog, take him into the hut and at night, kill him, dispose of the skin and insides, and cook the rest of his little carcass. I think that the dog must have had some presentiment of his doom, for try as we would he could not be enticed through to our side of the wire. We whistled and coaxed, but all the to no end, he kept a respectful distance away and at last with a delighted yap he bounded off back again in the direction he had come. We looked after him with a feeling of woe at his unleashed liberty. If only we could roam like that.

Wednesday 16th October 1918

Against the decision made on the 13th, our sub-committee obtain permission to go to Breslau, in search of a piano. They departed in high spirits to a few hours freedom in town, accompanied by two trusted guards.

They took with them all the proceeds of the sale of sacrificed cigarettes, namely 260 marks, thinking that in this country where piano's were manufactured that they ought to be rather cheap. But on arriving in the town they discovered that the cheapest they could obtain would cost 1600 marks. Of course that cancelled the idea altogether, so they returned empty handed. It was then definitely decided to erect the proposed memorial in the form of a broken fluted column for which a plan had been submitted by a local architect (whether this was ever done I could not say).

Thursday 17th October 1918

After all the usual proceedings of the day had been gone through and after our dinner of cabbage water we were all resting in the hut when in came a French Sergeant and speaking very good English, he enquired if it was possible for any of our boys to bargain with him for chocolate, or any kind of foodstuffs in exchange for really good cigarettes. He explained to us, that he and a few more of his comrades had been planning and were practically ready for their escape, and it only required a few odds and ends to complete their equipment. He was successful in a small degree in getting a few biscuits, bully beef, etc, so he departed quite happy after having told us all there was to tell about how they intended to get away. In all somewhere about 100 French had succeeded in getting away across the border into Austria, no doubt they would still be in enemy hands, but it was supposed that treatment was much better than that in Germany.

My grandfather is clearly disorientated by all his travels here, as Austria is some considerable distance from Lamsdorf.
Whilst not noted in his diary, the sergeant actually sent a postcard 20th October 1918 which follows, wherein he wrote:

My Dear Mother, just a line to let you know that I am still in the very best of health, hoping that all at home are same. I was rather surprised to receive a letter from you dated August 5th, and I am sorry that I did not come to see you now the last time I was on leave but unfortunately I was misguided by some individual it seems who has no very great liking for you, but never the less is my intention to fathom this business on my return to the old country, as I have been informed since then how things stood at that time and of this, "seeing is believing" with me this future. Well mother if you are desirous of sending me anything all I can ask for is tobacco, St Bruno, please as Francis has sent everything else I require. I will continue this next week so just tabs and tobacco. Your Loving Son. Will xxxxxx

The card was delivered 27ᵗʰ November 1918.

Sgt. Thomas William Chisholm

Monday 21ˢᵗ October 1918

There has been nothing very important happened within the last four days so I propose to skip over them which brings us to 21ˢᵗ October 1918 when a consignment of Emergency Parcels arrive in camp. After all had been opened each two men were given, 1 tin Milk, 1 tin Machonachin Rations, 2 pieces of sugar, 1 tin Veal loaf, 3 small biscuits, 2 spoons full of cocoa and tea and 4 cigarettes. So, happy with this present we went back to our hut for another good meal, as we no sooner got anything like this than it was eaten straight away.

Thursday 24ᵗʰ October 1918

Today our Serbian friend from the Eastern Front tries to get us some decent clothing by approaching the camp commandant but is refused, and very nearly put into cells for his pains, but he says that he does not care as the British people were always good to him.

How this Serbian got here was a miracle. He was taken prisoner right away down on the Eastern Front fighting against the Bulgars, and after being taken he took three British Tommies into his confidence and it appears that in pre-war days he was in the Isle of Man, but on the outbreak of war he tried to join the British

Army, but was refused and was sent to an internment camp for a short time. After a while he was sent back to his own country, where he still found it very hard to even get into his own army, owing to the fact no doubt that he had been away so long. However finally he was taken in and sent up to the front only to be taken prisoner along with a few British troops clad only in there khaki drill. Eventually with the help of this Serb, they made their escape at night and going across country the Serb was successful in blowing up an ammunition train on its way to the front. After this traveling by night and hiding during the day, he gets food for the party by purporting to be one of the German soldiers. After about eight days they were finally caught and landed up in our camp, almost dead from starvation and exposure to cold. He was without doubt a hero and looked upon as such by all in our camp. He could speak three or four different languages as good as any native, which eventually got him a job as an interpreter. Later he was doomed to be left in the camp all by himself after all the British had returned home.

Also this morning it had been arranged that three members of the committee belonging to Lager 3A should visit the cook house to see and inspect the place where our soup was boiled. This visit had been very difficult to arrange owing to the unwillingness of the camp Kommandant, for he seemed to think that we were incapable of looking after ourselves. However we succeeded at last, and at 10am off went our three members, taking with them the empty soup tubs that had contained our breakfast soup. Of course we were all under the impression that if we could only get on the good side of our guards we would be able to do a great deal more for our own personal comforts, but they always seemed unapproachable, as if we were dangerous and people to be watched with every move we made, so our attempts were very unsatisfactory indeed. In this direction our deputation to the cook house didn't improve the situation, for when they returned to the compound it was in a hurry.

It appeared that all went well, the building itself was a first class place containing all that would be desired by a squad of good cooks, but when they entered one compartment and noticed one of the cooks, who was of Russian nationality, stoking up the fires with coal, when he had done that, he was seen lifting up the lid of the huge boiler and commenced to stir up the contents with the same shovel. That ended all our chances of getting British cooks or better grub because he made one smack at the Russian and floored him straight away. That ended the inspection and he was promptly seized, marched back to be put in front of the Kommandant and given a good strapping for his pains and told that under no circumstances would any suggestion from the British be entertained again.

We were very much surprised indeed that he had not been put into cells, but we heard afterwards that the Kommandant had a little feeling of respect for our troops and this was a little comforting, and gave us a little more confidence in our position.

Friday 25th October 1918

Today I am issued with a biscuit ration, numbering 10 in all, so after boring a few holes in the tops and pouring in a good deal of water, put them in the sun to mature as it were. We three pals soon made short work of them.

The soup today was rotten, in fact it was not fit for human consumption, but it had to go down all the same and when the time came to turn in for the night, Fred pulled out a turnip and dividing it between the three, we munched it like a cow chewing the cud.

Saturday 26th October 1918

This is the first anniversary of our attack on Houthulst Forest last year when I was slightly wounded in the right knee and upper lip.

Sgt. Thomas William Chisholm

Sunday 27th October 1918

The usual visit to the Stable Church, and then back. Then I received a letter from home dated 22nd September.

(As you may be able to work out from a postcard displayed later, he may have been scolded in the letter he talks of here, because he apparently did not visit his mother during his only leave early in 1918.)

Monday 28th October 1918

Same old routine as usual but I arrange to go out to work in the forest again and when everyone is at work and the guards have settled down by the wagon, four of our party including myself sneak away to our treasure trove for another supply of potatoes and we succeed in getting about two stones.

There are rumours that an Armistice is about to take place and that gives us all something to speculate about as to what will happen here, but when we get back to camp it dies a natural death as usual.

Sgt. Thomas William Chisholm

Wednesday 30th October 1918

I got 4 postcards from home dated 26th, 27th, 30th, 31st July. It has taken them sometime to reach me, however they are most welcome.

At last we have discovered a method of dealing with our troublesome lodgers, for it has been part of our daily routine, what is commonly called a "chatting parade" which generally lasted for about two and a half hours, of course it was absolutely impossible to keep ourselves clean, owing to the treatment meted out to us on our last visit to the baths, and we rather preferred to retain our growth than go for another dose.

The weather by now being pretty cold, it was found that by divesting ourselves of our clothes at night and leaving such articles of clothing out in the very cold night air, that it had the effect of dispersing the creeper for a short while anyway, which gave us a little period of rest from scratching holes in our bodies. During the summer months when the weather was very hot, we used to sit for hours watching the comings and goings of the ants, many of which were nested close to the wooden walls of the hut. Their work was so regular that they had a real beaten track from one little hole in the ground to the other, so we discovered that by placing our clothes over the ant heaps, they would swarm over a shirt and attack the vermin in such a manner, that our freedom from torment was assured for about 24 hours. Of course there not being sufficient ant heaps for everybody's requirements, we all had to take turns of using one particular heap.

Chapter 10

November, More Rumours of Peace and an Armistice.

Sunday 4th November 1918

Again Fred and I go out to the forest to work, whilst Billy has to go to Lamsdorf railhead to work. When the day is over we pool all our goods, Billy has got about 3lbs of ground maize, Fred 3 turnips, and I a few potatoes so we make up a thick stew with the lot. One of the boys in the foraging party managed to stand on a baby rabbit whist returning to camp but it got away. I never felt more like doing murder than on this occasion, because the thought of what a nice tasty meal it would have made and we were so very hungry.

It is rumoured that peace is going to be declared, and that we will all be home before Xmas.

Oh, let it be soon."

Wednesday 6th November 1918

A large consignment of Red Cross parcels arrive today and I even see one with my name on, but I am unable to get it."

Sgt. Thomas William Chisholm

Thursday 7th November 1918

We have a very bad day today owing to one or two escapes during the night, the camp Kommandant had had all the guards paraded and gave them a good strapping for allowing such a thing to happen, and threatened all manner of punishments to them it ever happened again. Of course that meant they were in a very bad mood for the rest of the day and we suffered terribly for it. It appears that somewhere about 3-4am three Romanians had managed to cut the barbed wire in the vacinity of the British quarters and had succeeded in crawling through the hole under cover of darkness and made off in the direction of the mountain range to the east of the camp. They did not get far, because at 9am a posse of Germans came back with two of their number, the third had been shot whilst only a short way from the camp. We all felt very sorry for them indeed. Not only that but five Italians had also got away and could not be traced at all so we wished them all good luck. I think our French friends would be biting their fingers because they had planned to make their attempt sometime this week, but now it would be out of the question owing to the extra vigilance of the guards, who were doubled at night to prevent any recurrence.

I myself suffered individually at about 11am, Fred and I were lying in the grass by the main road leading up to our compound when up came a dapper little guard shouting "Englander here come for Arbitz Lause." and a good bit of language which we took to be swearing at us. We refused to move on this occasion because we all hated this particular man for more reasons than one, for he had made everyone's life an absolute hell whenever he got the chance. When we did not get up immediately, he just about boiled over, his face went all colours with rage, he lifted his heavy boot and let me have the full force of it, catching me on the very bottom of my spine. "Vass Englander hix lause, lause." he shouted. Although I suffered acute pain from his kick, I merely grinned at him which put the cap on things altogether, for he whipped out his bayonet, it was one of the saw edged type and slashed me across the back. Having just a paper thin jacket and shirt on the teeth easily penetrated so we thought it was then time to move before things got worse. Rising amid a storm of vile abuse from the guard, we made off to our compound as quickly as we possibly could, but not before telling him we would report him to the Kommandant for his conduct to a British NCO. However we did not do whatever work he wanted doing.

After bathing my wounds which proved to be three small punctures of the skin, we kept to the hut out of the way for the rest of the day.

Sgt. Thomas William Chisholm

Saturday 9th November 1918

There are very strong rumours of an armistice going round today, and everyone in camp are very excited about it, nothing is definitely gained so far as information is concerned. Our guards seem to be very vague on the matter, they tell us that they believe that Von Hindenberg and Count Ludendorff are to meet General Gough at Headquarters on the Western front, but that is all we are able to gather, so we just console ourselves with visions of an early release, and departure for our beloved England. Mainly the talk is about when we will get a decent meal because hunger is playing havoc amongst us. Owing to our reduced healthy conditions, our ribs are showing through the skin, jaws are sunken till the cheek bones seem to be coming through altogether and the sides of the stomach feel as if they are flapping together like sails in the wind. What an empty dreary feeling it is, the result being that life seems to become void of interest and nothing is left for us but to wish for death to take us out of it all.

Sgt. Thomas William Chisholm

Sunday 10th November 1918

A very memorable day this will ever be. It dawns very cold, wet and dreary, as winter already has set its grip upon the land. Black frosts occur at night and it is almost impossible to sleep, as we have as stated earlier, only two small badly worn blankets, alive with vermin.

Orders arrive that there is to be no church service, no reason is given, and the air seems to be full of mystery.

We are paraded as usual for the daily count, and after that told to dismiss, but not to go very far away. It never was our intention to wander very far in case there happened to be any chance of any food whilst we were away, because something to feed our famished bellies was always uppermost in our minds.

So far as a smoke, well we had long since resorted to the manufacture of our own mixture, which we invariably changed from time to time. Sometimes we gathered from round about the outside of the compound some nice blades of grass, also loads of clover, and after drying them thoroughly, mix up the two and smoke them as best we could. Sometimes mixing a few dried tea leaves if they were obtainable, of course when we did have tea, the leaves were never thrown away. They were always kept smuggled away in a tin box for when we wanted a smoke.

Today however, to while away a little bit of time, Fred and I decided to walk as far as the main entrance to the camp, so with our paper jacket collars turned up about the neck, shoulders haunched forward and hands behind our backs, we trudged or slouched along the road very slowly. Nothing was done very quickly in case it passed too soon and we were left with nothing to do. Reaching the main gate everything seemed very normal outwardly, but in the Scheibstube or office, which was a substantially built hut placed inside the gates, things seemed to be humming. Being more or less used to the excitable nature of the German soldier we took no notice of this, and turning about started to make our way back to the compound.

When only half of the journey had been made we discovered that something very unusual was going on, for walking round on the raised bank of earth which served as the sentries beat, was a soldier with an armful of newspapers. This had never been done before so naturally we though it very peculiar. When he arrived at the sentry nearest to our compound and also the hut occupied by the guard, he stopped, presented a paper to the sentry on duty and had a good talk with him in a very hard voice, and waving his arms all over the place like a human windmill, and then continued his journey.

Fred and I watched for a what was going to happen next, and it did suddenly, for with a scowl on his face fit to make it crack, he unslung his rifle and flung it on the ground at his feet, then taking off his helmet, and placing his fingers under the eagle which was his badge, he viciously tore it away and flung it across the field. To say the least we began to get a little nervous, but couldn't move, we seemed to be rooted to the spot, next he tore out the collar patches from his jacket, then stamping along to the next sentry, they both had consultation, and returning to the guard hut were joined by all the other guards.

So, there we were, with absolutely no one on guard over us at all, when things reached this stage we thought it time to get back into our hut as quickly as possible in case anything detrimental happened to us. Just at that critical moment there come up the road three British Officers, and entering our compound called all the British soldiers together. There were not many of us left now as a good many had died, so it was not a big gathering that he addressed.

THE NEWS IS BROKEN

As I have already explained the huts were built so that only about two feet was above ground level, so the smaller man of the three, who turned out to be a medical officer, mounted onto the top of the centre hut and commenced to address the assembled men. "Well men I can see that you are all in a very poor condition, but nevertheless, it will not be for very long now, as I have some very good news for you. First of all you will have noticed the very unusual behavior of your guards today. I might warn you that this may develop into a very ugly situation, so pay particular attention to what I am about to say. An armistice has been declared. From today you are free men, free to go where and when you please. In a few moments more the prison camp gates will be thrown open to you, but I do not want you to go. Please stay where you are for the present anyhow. Whatever you do, don't mix with the other nationalities, for in all probability they will take advantage of the chance to go free, and go mad. They might prove to be dangerous, so stay where you are. A revolution has broken out in the country, the Kaiser has abdicated, and the Crown Prince has renounced his right to the position held by his father, so you see what may happen if you go wandering about the country. You are too far inland to be able to get to any seaport within a reasonable time, and furthermore you would be unable to get any food en-route. So you see how advisable it is to stay where you are. These two brother officers and I are going to take command of you and do whatever we

125

can for your welfare, so far as better food and accommodation is concerned. Don't be alarmed at what is going on behind you, I don't think they will fire."

When we looked round there were eight or nine guards with their rifles leveled at us. However we stood our ground, and one of the officers went across and spoke to them, and they dispersed, being satisfied that we were not going to cause any disturbance.

The M.O. then said that he would get us moved as soon as he could get in touch with the camp Kommandant, then raising his hand as if to give a blessing he quoted:

> God alone be with us now,
> Lest we forget
> Lest we forget.

Then he came down and talked to us for a good while. The other two officers belonged to the R.N.D and the Buffs, and before he went away, he asked us to sing the national anthem, which was readily done, although everyone had a lump in their throat and tears of joy in their eyes.

Thus ended one day that will always be remembered by anyone that was in that camp.

Sgt. Thomas William Chisholm

Monday 11th November 1918

Similar to yesterday the weather is cold and dreary, but we hardly notice it as we are so interested in the present situation. The troops who have been our guards so long, are busy packing, rolling up blankets and various other duties connected with moving from one place to another.

After a breakfast of brown soup with five grains of barley in the bottom (I have counted them), we are all called out on parade, counted and ordered to march. The half dead column moved out of the compound and down the main roadway in the direction of the main gate. Arriving at the main gate a halt is called, when we are all closed right up and counted again, the gate is opened and we move off towards Lager One, which is also in the direction of the station. Of course all sorts of suggestions are put forward as to where we are bound for. One fellow said home, but he was soon told to shut up, and not to talk so daft. However we finally arrived in Lager One and lined up in front of the stores where we were issued with:

1 Handkerchief (Khaki)
1 Towel (between two men)
1 Razor, shaving brush and soap (between three men)

Very happy with this additional comfort we marched back to Lager Three A to get busy with these implements and our first shave in nearly eight months.

The Republican flag is hoisted on the camp flagstaff amid cheers from a few Germans assembled to witness the ceremony, but this did not affect our troops in any way, for they went about in their usual manner.

Great excitement occurred this afternoon on the arrival of five hundred and sixteen Red Cross Parcels from Lager One. "Surely there will be one amongst them all for us." said I. "Lets hope so, God knows we could do with it." said Fred.

We are advised that the Germans are getting ready a number of transports, which are due to start within the next three weeks and in confirmation of this, certain of our men are detailed to take all people who are still suffering from wounds across to the hospital, in readiness for the first transport. This gives us a bright outlook, and cheers us up.

Gerry did not move today.

Monday 12th November 1918

Consternation and indignation were fully evident very early this morning, for on awakening it was discovered that almost every box that anyone possessed in our hut, had been either rifle, or stolen altogether.

These boxes of course were made by the men themselves more for pastime than anything else, and made from any kind of wood possible from anywhere and in most cases were the result of very hard work, because not being in possession of tools of any kind, sometimes took weeks to make.

In most cases the wood came from the boxes containing biscuits from Berlin, and after the box had been emptied, we then proceeded with the task of planning the best way to make the article that we should be proud of. First it was carefully pulled to pieces, care being taken not to split any of the pieces, also not to lose any of the nails, for they were very precious. Next the size and shape was decided, then followed the work of cutting and shaving each piece to fit closely to the other. All the cutting was done with a small penknife. When this had been carefully executed, came the work of putting the pieces together. Having no hammers we were obliged to use a piece of stone, which was a very awkward tool indeed, and resulted in a good many valuable nails being bent, rendering them useless. However we all carried on as best we could and when the main part of the box had been built, next came the work of putting on the lid. There was nothing so common as the ordinary flat lid with battens across the inside. It had to be made box fashion, about one and a half inches deep, and when it had been made in the rough and fitted, probably it would not lie level or fit as close as desired it would be taken outside, and on the cement foundation, the wooden edges of the box would be scrubbed until they were perfectly level, and the lid fitted close. When this had been done, we made hinges out of old empty tins found lying about. This was the most difficult part, but after cutting and a lot of hacking at the piece of tin, a pair of hinges took shape. Finally with a piece of scrap wire, a staple and hasp were made and the box complete, and our meager possessions were put in.

As I said before, nearly all had been stolen or rifled. How had it been done? No one could explain, for it must have been done very quietly indeed. We decided in stockinged feet. There was a concerted rush for the door in the hope of catching anyone going through the stolen boxes outside, not having the patience to wait until they got back to their own part of the camp, but no one was visible. However, just outside the hut door we found an Italians hat, so we decided that it was the Italians who had committed the outrage.

To say the least, if we had only seen one Italian in possession of any of our goods at that moment there would have been murder done on the spot, because all our belongings were in them, including the small amounts of biscuits, or bully beef that we had.

After a search round one or two compounds we found a few of the boxes smashed up, open, and the contents strewn all over the ground minus any part of foodstuffs. However they didn't get any food from mine, and when it was found behind our own hut, all that had been in was soaked for it had rained that night. We all decided to take it quietly and wait until someone put themselves away and then we would take action. However nothing more was found out, or heard of about the affair.

Tuesday 19th November 1918

Six days have elapsed without anything of importance taking place. On rising this morning we were greeted with a good covering of snow, the air was clear and crisp but two days earlier we could see the snow on the tops of the mountains, so we were not surprised.

Chapter 11

December, Still Not Home Yet.

Sunday 1st December 1918

"A Plot Revealed

One sergeant arrived back in camp at dinner time from working at the railhead, in the company of a squad of Russians. He had relieved a Tommy of his jacket earlier that morning in the hope of exchanging it for a bit of salt fish or ground meal. However he brought news of an intended raid on the British quarters by a mob of Russians.

It appeared that he had heard them talking together and one of the guards had told him what the conversation was about, and he came to us with the warning. Not wishing for a repeat of the happenings of the 12th, we immediately took steps to fortify ourselves against any possible attack. Anything we could use as a weapon was kept by our beds, and when finally we retired for the night it was agreed to barricade the door. When the doors had been closed for the night, we moved one of the sets of bunks right close up and with what rope we could get hold of, securely fastened the door to the posts of the bunk, because the doors happened to open outward. It was seen that if anyone tried to open them, as soon as they were pulled, the bunks would shake and wake the occupants, thus we would be warned in time to defend ourselves.

Of course this was not done just in fear of losing our goods, but in all probability of saving life, because we knew that the Russians were in a desperate plight from want of food, and they would not hesitate to kill if necessary. So we were obliged to take these precautions.

However, nothing came to pass that night, but we continued this practice for something like a week. All the time during the day we had them visiting our hut for any soup which was not used up, but we always kept a wary eye on them and would not permit them to come further than the inside of the door.

Monday 2nd December 1918

A batch of prisoners from another camp called Munster arrived today, amongst them being an Irish corporal of my own platoon. The joy of our meeting again, is almost impossible to imagine.

I think we remained out of bed more than half the night talking over all that had happened in our various stages of captivity.

He told me that he had been kept behind the lines during the first three months, engaged in carrying wounded back to the dressing station. Before returning to the front line they were made to hump shells and ammunition.

They were only given one meal per day, until he was nothing but a skeleton and thoroughly run down. They were then obliged to send this batch of now useless men right into Germany. Had this not been done they would all have died from starvation and overwork, not counting the ill treatment.

However we had been given Emergency Parcels today, so I shared what I could afford with him, and he seemed very grateful when he retired to sleep.

Tuesday 3rd December 1918

During the night shots were heard at intervals, telling us that it is either more attempted escapes, or prowling wolves.

In going out next morning for soup, we are just in time to see three guards marching two Romanians back into camp. They had escaped during the night, and had made for the village about 2 miles south west of the camp, in an endeavour to steal bread from the local bakery. They'd have succeeded very well, had they not been caught. They each carried a sack containing six loaves in each, but these were confiscated on arrival at the camp.

Thursday 5th December 1918.

Today being a very wet day, there was no work done, and nothing happened, but on the morning of the 6[th,] notices were posted in the work house, as to the movement of British troops from various camps.
This made things look a bit more rosey.

Saturday 7th December 1918

Another two Romanians are brought back into camp this morning.

The Medical Officer, who had come to the camp, has been busy trying to get better living quarters for us and the first stage takes place today at 10.00am. He arrives at the compound in the company of a number of high officials to inspect the camp in general, and they went through every hut. On coming to the last one, the Chief was overheard to remark "It's amazing, I don't know how the poor fellows have lived so long in these huts. I will see what can be done to have them removed to a better place as soon as I get back to Berlin, in fact, I will send a wire".

In one part of this last hut, the side is bulging in and moisture is running through. It is from the latrine just outside, about 6 feet away from the window. As no proper places had been built, what was done, was to dig a large hole 12 feet long by 8 feet across, and 10 to 15 feet deep. Across the top of this hole length ways, were placed four planks of wood to act as seating, where we were obliged to go to do any business needed. Eventually these sumps becoming so full, that the earth between not being strong enough to withhold the strain, it took the least line of resistance, and found its way into the huts, and the smell being so foul, it was almost impossible to live there.

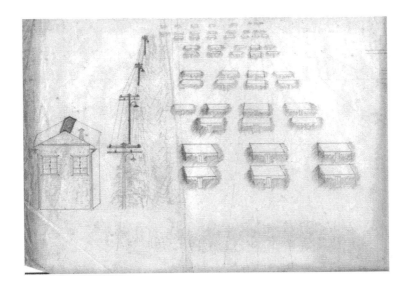

Remember the Sergeant has previously described the huts as being sunken into the ground with about two feet only above ground

level. The drawing above is a photograph of the Sergeants sketch of the huts along with a guardhouse, the wire fence and ditch.

This afternoon it was reported that the Italian prisoners were catching rats, and eating them as they were so hungry.

Monday 9th December 1918

Another delegation came and inspected the camp this morning, this time from Breslau.

They say that they had no idea that we were living in such squalor, and shocking conditions. It is about this time, that we learn that this camp was condemned for the habitation of British prisoners of war in its early day of existence.

Tuesday 10th December 1918

Following this inspection the MO tells us that yet another lot of officials are coming to inspect the camp. On this occasion they are coming from Berlin, so things seem to be moving along fairly well towards the promised removal to better barracks.

Let it be soon we all say together.

Sgt. Thomas William Chisholm

Wednesday 11th December 1918

Early this morning the Major from the RhD comes on parade and proceeded to organize our troops into some sort of composite battalion, and is very successful. He arranged that, to save the removal of any of our belongings, that each two huts should form one Company, irrespective as to what Regiment a man belonged to.

So here we are another step forward to better times, also with a much better supply of food, things where looking more rosy.

Another surprise came to us in the afternoon, for soon after dinner, we were ordered to fall in by Companies with all our belongings, in readiness to move. Sure enough by 3.30pm we were vacating the old huts for proper barracks in Lager 5.

On arrival there, we were put into good huts, with the men in the large part, and Sgt's in the cubicles at the further end. They were furnished with about 8 bunks, a large stove, chairs and a table which made these places more like a palace, compared with what we had just left.

The Sergeants drawing of the layout of the much improved conditions he talks about above, which they found with their move to Lager 5 hut.

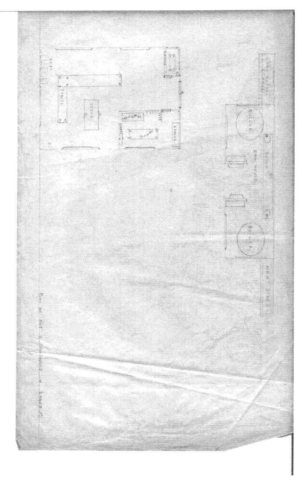

With this move, we felt like we were actually out of German hands and management, and that we were absolutely under British rule.

We had a great sing song that night before going to bed.

Thursday 12th December 1918

Today has been spent in getting into the camp as many British Red Cross Parcels as possible and it has been arranged that before distribution all goods such as tea, cocoa, bully beef, sugar and any other things that could be used in the cook house, (for we had to have cooks on duty) so that the cooks could make them up into a decent meal. So after these articles had been extracted, we were at liberty to have as much bread, margarine, dripping, cheese, biscuits, cigarettes and tobacco as we liked and really what we do get is far in excess of our present requirements, because each man now is issued every day with:

> Two loaves of milk bread,
> One tin of Cheese,
> One tin of dripping,
> One pound of Huntley & Palmers Biscuits
> Four Packets of Woodbines,
> One tin Margarine,

One tin Jam.

These of course were only the dry goods, after that came the tea and stores which was the cooks part in the programme, so we are not taking any harm.

Strict orders have been issued from Battalion Headquarters that under no circumstances is any food to be sold or given to the German troops, but it was needless to make such a decree after the treatment they had given us. Never the less we had plenty of beggars round at all times of the day and I felt that I should like to do something desperate.

In the evening we go down to Lager 1 to a cinema show, it is to be in aid of the memorial which we are going to erect to our pals before we leave Germany. It proved to be a fairly good show, excepting that all the titles and the reading on the screen were in German so we failed to follow the pictures, also we were not allowed to smoke as notices were painted in two places either side of the stage "Rauchend ist Verbotten".

After the show, a party of six, of which I was one, adjourned to a small pub and had a sample of Beck Beer. This was forced through the pumps by the use of gas from a cylinder alongside the small counter.

In the far corner of the room, sat a party of Gerry troops drinking and singing to the music supplied by a melodeon, which was played by one of the party.

Altogether everything seemed to be in a happy state, but sometimes we were the recipients of some vicious glances from them, but we took not the slightest notice of them for we were free men now, and didn't care for all the German notions, till one of our party voiced that view, and then we thought it was time to get a move on in case it came to something worse, so we went back to camp, had a good supper of stew, and highly satisfied with our days work, went to bed to dream of the day when we should be aboard the train for merry England.

Sunday 15th December 1918

Today after a short parade and inspection by our C.O. we were dismissed and just wandered about the camp as we pleased. Our path took us into a German canteen which by appearances was used by all and sundry, as included in its customers were a few children, poorly fed, and poorly clad. They were really in a very poor state altogether, which only went to show once more the ravages of war on the younger generations.

It must take a long time to make things up to pre-war standards again.

Sgt. Thomas William Chisholm

Monday 16th December 1918

A large consignment of clothing arrived from Lager 1, to equip the men of the first transport. We had a very busy day, but I was doomed to disappointment, for when the list of names was read over, my name failed to appear, so Fred and I were very gloomy at having to be separated after all our times of strife together, for he was down to go with this first batch.

However we had to make the best of things, so I helped him to pack his few goods and get him ready.

After that we turned out for a smoke and a wander round the huts, before turning in for the night.

Wednesday 18th December 1918.

I am on duty today as Orderly Sergeant to the camp and receive an order that at 7:15pm tonight there are to be four guides per company, at the main gate in readiness to meet a batch of men coming in from another camp.

So it came about, that Fred and I parted company on this night, and I was to welcome into the camp 950 new arrivals, who in all probability would also go before I did, so I had to cover up my misery and carry on.

Sgt. Thomas William Chisholm

Thursday 19th December 1918

It's my birthday, I am 22 today and I am very miserable indeed, for I had thought to spend it in dear old England, but not so, however I had a talk with the cooks and it ended up with a nice little spread in our hut where we celebrated very well indeed under the circumstances.

There are rumours again of another transport on Sunday to include in it all cripples and every two days after that.

Tuesday 24th December 1918

As a special treat today we have been given a large amount of sausage from the Germans, but I may say that very little of it was eaten as we have any amount of our own food now. I suppose that this was sent as a peace offering owing to it being Xmas eve. Also included in the gift were two packets of tobacco and a Xmas card. The tobacco proved only to be dried oak leaves, and the card we discovered had been intended for one in England, for on the side used for correspondence, were the words "Printed in Germany", but on the picture side the greeting was in German.

Sgt. Thomas William Chisholm

Sunday 29th December 1918.

Orders are issued that the camp must be closed by the 1st January 1919. The excitement is great and we all start packing our little wooden boxes in readiness for the journey.
Then we wait.

Monday 30th December 1918.

Still we wait.

Tuesday 31st December 1918

The day begins as usual, and still we wait.

In the evening orders are issued that all officers, NCO's and men will parade outside the orderly room at 2pm tomorrow dressed ready for marching off, greatcoat and one blanket over the arm. I might say that all men were ready before the appointed time, but when we did parade and were just about to march off, it was found that there was one man to be left in the camp. That one man was our Serbian friend who had been so useful to us since his arrival. We pleaded with our officers to allow him to come back with us, but we were informed that if we did take him, he would not be allowed to land in England, and would only have to come back again and then as things were just now, he was nearer his own country and no doubt the Germans would see to his comfort alright.

Chapter 12

January 1919, God Bless HMS Concord and the Royal Navy.

Wednesday 1st January 1919

So finally we were marched off, and at Lamsdorf station boarded the train.

A different kind of train it was this time, none of the cattle trucks which we came here in, but instead real carriages with properly upholstered seats. So with eight men in a carriage we rolled away in the direction of a seaport on the Baltic Sea called Stettin.

At the end of our train were two vans with two days supply of food which was issued at intervals along the route, so taking no harm until our arrival at Stettin, where we left the train, lined up in fours, and marched along the docks until rounding the corner of a warf to a wonderful greeting from British sailors of H.M.S Royal Navy on board H.M.S Concord. They were evidently expecting our arrival judging by the rousing cheers that filled the air, and also our hearts with unbounded joy. It really seemed like a strange dream, almost unbelievable and we felt afraid to even rub our eyes in case it was so.

The ships band had turned out on the forward deck, and I think they played their instruments as they had never been played before, and this mob of ours seemed too full to cheer, for it was a very weak attempt that was made for there were tears of joy in everyone's eyes.

We were immediately allowed to file on board, the Sergeants being ordered to fall out to one side until all the men were on board, and finally when it came to our turn we were placed in quarters with the Royal Marines.

We had not been on board a quarter of an hour when it was announced that a meal was ready for us and would we please be seated. Well it all seemed too good to be true, for on sitting down to a beautiful table with snow white cloth, and on that cloth a bottle of Bass beer, also a plate with roast beef, green peas, potatoes and Yorkshire puddings. It is impossible to define our feelings, we did not need any second invitation to eat, but were told to go steady because after the utter starvation we had experienced in the last few months, it would perhaps not agree with us it we gorged ourselves, which we felt very much like doing.

The marines waited on us as if we were lords and were very kind to us indeed, in fact one would imagine that we were the actual people who had ended the war for them. After a good meal, one of the Corporals of the marines seemed to take to me, and asked if I would care to have a look over the ship from top to bottom, I say that because we started at the fighting top, or crows nest as it is sometimes called, working by stages and all the while the Corporal showing me how this worked and what this and that was for and so and so, and altogether it was a very interesting tour. On our return to quarters we were just in time to partake in an issue of rum, so having taken my ration I wandered up on to the after deck, because after this time we had moved off and were speeding down the river Oder, and I wished to see all that was to be seen while the chance lasted.

By this time it was getting dusk, so I took up my post up against one of the gun turrets, because by this time that small bottle of beer, and the rum ration together were beginning to have their effect on me, and I was feeling a little unsteady, however I interested myself in one of the officers standing beside this particular turret, who with a large sketch book was rapidly sketching everything along the banks of that river. He just seemed to take a glance well ahead and start work with his pencil and almost before we were level with his object he had everything down in detail. He was a very clever man indeed.

There is a painting by Leiutenant Cecil King of the prisoners boarding HMS Concord in the port of Stettin 1st January 1919, which I would have liked to have included here, as my Grandfather would have been one of the soldiers featured in the painting, but it could not be displayed here. However it can be viewed on the Imperial War Museums website and is listed as IWM ART 2692 in their collections as item object 15304.

Night came upon us, and it was time to turn in, so my friend the Corporal gave up his hammock for my use, and others followed his example. After undressing I made an attempt to climb into it, but try as I may I failed each time, amid roars of laughter from the crew. It really was funny to see about twenty or so men endeavouring to get into those hammocks. At last the Corporal assisted me in and pulling the beautiful white blankets over me, bid me a good nights sleep. I think it was the most comfortable bed I ever had slept in, for I hardly seemed to have been asleep two hours when it was time to get up again.

Thursday 2nd January 1919

I was just semi conscious when I was rudely awakened by a bump from under my hammock, and I found myself in the arms of three marines. They could hardly keep hold of me for laughing, they said that was the way they treated all sleepy heads in the navy. They normally allowed the culprit to fall onto the deck, but they put me down gently.

I proceeded to dress and get ready for breakfast which consisted of real bacon and real eggs. We had not seen an egg for nearly nine months, so it was quite a new thing to us, but first came a whacking big plate of porridge with plenty of milk and it made one really feel that after all it was good to be alive.

We travelled all day until about 10pm when we arrived in the dock at Copenhagen, here we left the ship, much against our wish, but the Commander said that his orders had to be obeyed and they were that we had to be left in Denmark for a short while. So we were put on board a train and moved off in the darkness to our new billets a few miles away.

The trains were of the double decker type, and whenever we came to a tunnel it seemed that the train must knock off it's top before it would be able to get through, but we got to the camp without such a mishap somewhere about 12:30am. Here we were just put into bunks by Danish soldiers anyhow, until the following morning, when we were sorted out and put into proper squads necessary for administration.

This ended our Prisoner of War life and after a month in Denmark we were returned to England to eventually be demobbed and what?

Sgt. Thomas William Chisholm